Eat Seasonally

Delicious Recipes for Spring, Summer, Fall, and Winter

CREATED BY

TRUVANI.

Table of Contents

Why Eat Seasonally	7
How To Get The Best Seasonal Produce	10
Spring	15
Spring Seasonal Spotlights	19
Spring Recipes	25
Summer	43
Summer Seasonal Spotlights	47
Summer Recipes	53
Fall	75
Fall Seasonal Spotlights	79
Fall Recipes	85
Winter	111
Winter Seasonal Spotlights	115
Winter Recipes	121

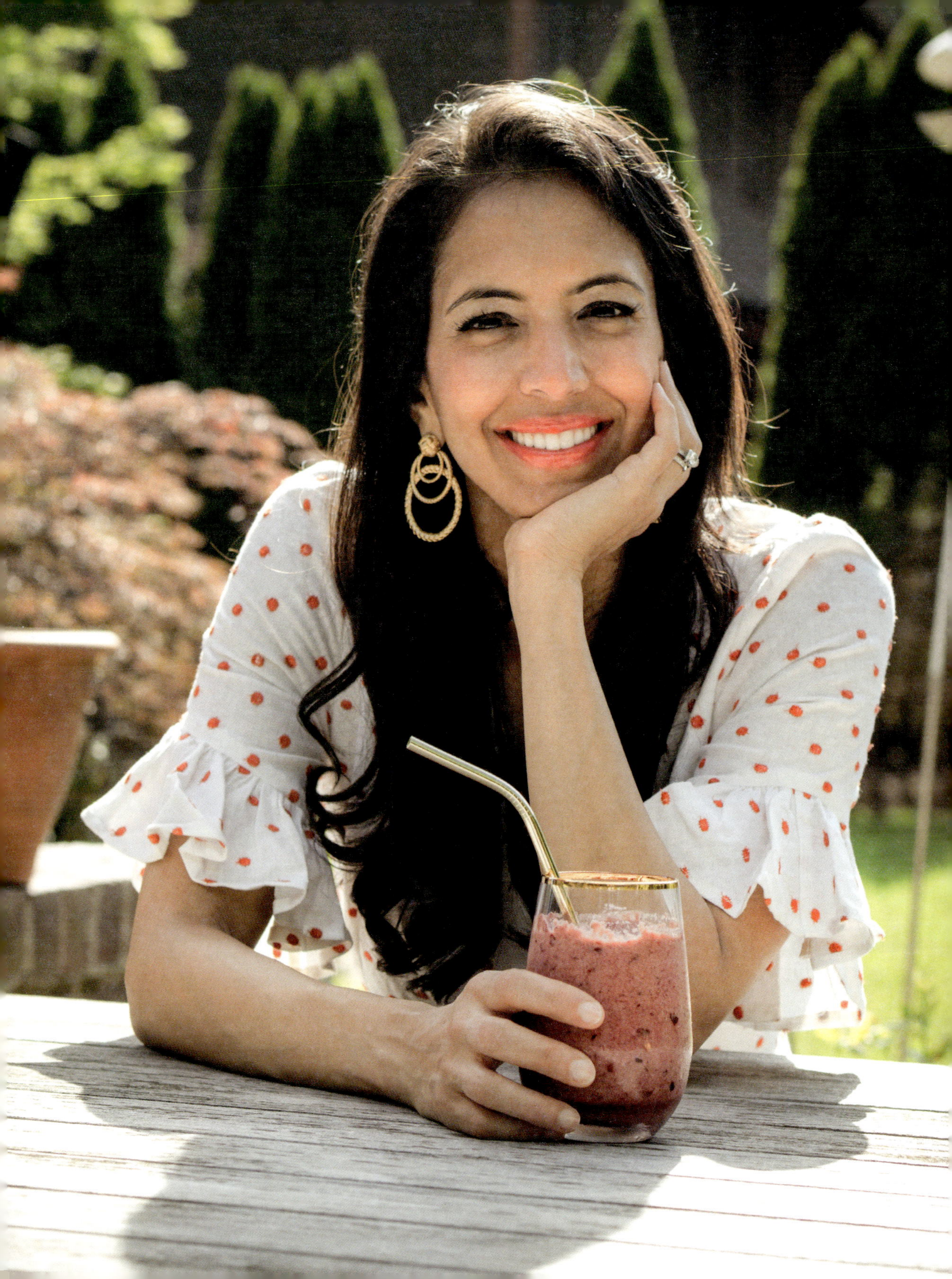

SOME OF MY FAVORITE MEMORIES ARE FROM SEASONAL HARVEST TIMES IN OUR HOME GARDEN.

My family and I love to gather fresh heirloom tomatoes off the vine for a summer Gazpacho. Or veggies like cucumber and peppers to throw into a grain bowl as a simple solution when friends stop by for dinner.

I also love heading to the local farmer's stand with no agenda — loading up on fresh veggies and herbs I've never seen so we can explore new recipes in the kitchen.

That's exactly what I wanted to offer in this guide. I invite you to explore seasonal cooking in a way that brings new flavors to your kitchen. You may run across ingredients you've never seen, or try recipes that become staples in your home.

This cookbook walks you through each season with recipes created and tested from our own Truvani community. Inside these pages you'll find fresh salads, hearty soups, flavorful dinners, and delightful desserts from Truvani fans who love food as much as I do.

I recommend bookmarking the recipes you can use each season. Though many of these ingredients can be found year round, it's better to shop when they are grown locally from farmers in your community. It's not only good for your own budget, but also the local economy and environment.

This beautiful book can be the centerpiece of your kitchen. No matter the time of year, something delicious will always be at your fingertips.

I hope you enjoy these recipes as much as my family and I do.

xo,
Vani

March
2020
April
2020
June
2020
August
2020
October
2020
December
January
2020

Why Eat Seasonally

Most grocery stores are stocked year-round with an assortment of fruits and vegetables. So there's nothing to stop you from making a warm hearty stew of potatoes and root vegetables for a Fourth of July picnic.

Or serving watermelon slices at Thanksgiving.

Deciding what to eat and when comes down to part intuition and part cultural tradition.

But there's a third factor that should come into play: intention.

If you want to eat in season, you have to intend to! You have to know what to look for, where to look, and you have to know what time of year is best for the foods you eat.

But why is eating seasonally important, and arguably superior, to just strolling the aisles of a grocery store and picking out what to eat non-discriminately?

YOU FIND BETTER QUALITY WHEN YOU EAT SEASONALLY

Have you ever thought about what it takes to indulge in a "fresh" peach in the middle of January?

Peaches come into season during the heat of summer. So if you find a ripe peach in February, it most likely means that peach was grown and harvested in the Southern Hemisphere.

Why does this affect quality?

To get a ripe peach in February, it needs to be picked well before it's ready so it doesn't rot while in transport. This alone dramatically affects quality and taste.

Then that peach needs to embark on a sizable journey to reach your grocer's produce section.

Just think about how long that peach probably sat on a loading dock. Or all the temperature fluctuations it endured. It's been stressed.

This affects quality, as well.

EATING SEASONALLY BOOSTS THE ECONOMY

When you're focused on eating seasonally, you'll quickly discover that the best finds - both in your grocery stores and farmer's markets - come from regional farms and businesses.

When you shop local, you're actively helping your regional economy. You're also contributing to a healthy job market, supporting local families, and making sure that your community is supported with services and programs.

EATING SEASONALLY IS MORE AFFORDABLE

When you choose to buy from local farms and businesses and eat seasonally, you can generally expect to pay less for quality food and produce.

While organic, fresh food has the reputation of being expensive and reserved for the affluent, the opposite is true when you shop smart (like at a local farmer's market).

Why is this?

Remember our story of the winter peach that had an epic journey halfway across the globe to get to the supermarket?

Well, we all know that traveling can be expensive, and the same is true for our food!

Importing food into the US is incredibly complicated and expensive. When you eat seasonally and shop local, you cut down the number of intermediaries there are in the process of acquiring your food.

And in many cases, you can buy directly from your farmers!

But when you buy off-season at the grocery store, the supply chain to get you those fruits and vegetables is long and expensive.

EATING SEASONALLY IS MORE SUSTAINABLE FOR THE ENVIRONMENT

Eating non-local, non-seasonal produce is not only expensive, but it's not nearly as sustainable as eating seasonally.

And for many of the same reasons too.

Transporting produce across the globe has a more significant impact on the environment than the pickup truck used to deliver CSA boxes or produce to the weekly farmer's market.

In addition, when you have the intention to eat seasonally, you're more likely to support smaller, organic farms. This is in contrast to the industrial farms used to grow and distribute produce globally for mass production throughout the year.

EATING SEASONALLY MEANS TASTIER, MORE NUTRITIOUS PRODUCE

When you intend to eat seasonally, you're more likely to choose organic produce that has been harvested at the right time.

If you've ever bitten into a fresh, perfectly ripe strawberry at the farmer's market or enjoyed a tomato picked straight from your garden for a summer salad, then you know this all too well.

Few things in life taste as wonderful as perfectly ripe, freshly harvested produce!

And as a bonus, produce consumed shortly after being harvested, and in the peak of ripeness, are more nutritionally dense than produce picked too early and left to ripen while in a cargo container.

The reason for this is two-fold:

1. When something is harvested too early, its flavor profile never fully develops. Even produce that continues to ripen after harvesting suffers this fate. All fruits and vegetables benefit from being picked when ready.

2. As soon as something is picked or harvested, it begins to lose nutritional value. This means you are much better off eating a cucumber straight from your garden versus one store-bought.

In summary, when you want to extract as much flavor and nutritional value from the foods you eat, as well as save money and contribute to your local economy, it's best to eat seasonally whenever possible!

How to Get The Best Seasonal Produce

We are lucky to live in a world where fresh, local fruits and vegetables are pretty easy to come by.

Grocery stores are increasingly adding local sections to their produce departments, but there are several other ways to acquire fresh, local produce. And some of these ways may surprise you!

SHOP YOUR LOCAL FARMER'S MARKET

Most larger towns and cities have a handful of well-known farmer's markets that people are aware of and shop at regularly.

These popular markets pop up in designated places regularly throughout the growing season and provide local residents with opportunities to buy fresh food and produce at affordable prices. You can find them in town squares, at local fairgrounds, and on main streets.

It's definitely worth your time to seek out and support these local markets.

But there are even more farmer's markets in existence than you're probably aware of. And they may be taking place in your local community right this minute.

We're talking about "micro" farmer's markets. These tiny enclaves of fresh fruit, vegetables, and homemade goods are the hidden gems where you can find the best selection and best prices on all things seasonal.

These markets can sometimes be found on the road-side, adjacent to the local farmer producer.

These markets can often be found in the back parking lots of churches, businesses, and community groups. These markets can often be pop-ups that only come to life a few times per year. The trick to finding these "micro" markets is to pay attention.

Local farmers are most likely not focused on updating their Google listings or Facebook Page, so many times, the main advertisement for these types of markets will not be found using Google or Facebook, but by reading church bulletins, local newspapers, word of mouth and listening to the radio.

CSA BOXES

CSA stands for Community Supported Agriculture. And CSA box programs are not only a convenient way to ENSURE you eat seasonally but being a CSA member can be both fun and affordable too!

When you sign up with a local farm to be a CSA Member, you commit to supporting that farm financially in exchange for receiving a share of their harvest.

It's a symbiotic relationship that many farms and families cannot live without.

When you become a CSA member, you help a local farmer stay in business, and in exchange for your support, you'll receive a box of fresh produce regularly throughout the growing season.

Now here's the fun part... You don't get to pick what's in the box!

Most CSA farms allow you to indicate a preference, but when you become a CSA member, you're raising your hand to say that:

- You want to support your local farmer
- You want to try a variety of fresh local fruits and vegetables, and
- You have an adventurous spirit and are willing to try new things!

Because here's a secret most people don't know about CSA farms and memberships.

Many CSA farms supply local grocery stores and restaurants with seasonal fruits and vegetables, and for the most part, they grow the type of produce that is expected in the market. But farmers are creative people, and they like to experiment and grow exotic or heirloom varieties of fruits and vegetables that most people in the grocery store wouldn't recognize!

So when you support a CSA farmer, you end up supporting their creative spirit and their desire to grow the unusual.

- You get the heirloom varieties of tomatoes and peppers and squash.
- You get the herbs you can't find at your local market.
- And you get the recipes they've experimented within their kitchen.

FINDING A LOCAL CSA TO SUPPORT

If you're interested in joining a CSA in your area, there are a couple of ways to find options available to you.

- Google "CSA" + your city or town. This should return a few good results.
- Ask your favorite restaurant that focuses on seasonal ingredients and farms. They have contacts that they're usually more than happy to share.
- Look on bulletin boards at your local natural food stores and markets
- Ask farmers that you meet at the farmer's market.

GROWING YOUR OWN PRODUCE AT HOME

If you've never attempted to grow your own food at home, you may be surprised by a few things:

- How little space is needed to experience your own seasonal bounty
- How much produce you'll get from a single plant!
- And how delicious and rewarding growing your own food can be

Whether you have a plot of land to dedicate to a garden or you're limited to a patio from your 3rd-floor condo, growing your own seasonal produce can be easier than you think.

FIRST, GROW FOOD YOU WILL EAT

Heirloom radishes and squash may sound fun, but will you and your family eat them? If yes, go for it, but if not, focus on the tried and true fruits and vegetables that you know your family will eat.

Think tomatoes, cucumbers, leafy greens, and peppers.

These are all easy veggies to grow that have a high yield when gardening in confined spaces.

And remember this: one tomato plant goes a long, long way! Same with things like cucumbers, peppers, and kale. You don't need rows and rows of one variety to feed your family. Often times one to two plants per garden is more than sufficient.

OBTAIN GREAT SOIL

When it comes to the soil to use for your garden, it's best to skip the options at Home Depot and to invest in the best dirt you can find.

We suggest seeking out a farm supply store and finding a quality compost to use. When you're growing food for just your family, you will not need much, and when it comes to quality, a little goes a long way.

USE CONTAINERS OR RAISED BEDS FOR YOUR GARDEN

Containers and raised beds make backyard gardening so much easier than planting and growing in the ground. You can control water, drainage, and nutrient levels so much better, making your efforts a lot more manageable.

BE PROACTIVE

Gardening involves troubleshooting. That's because there's simply no way to avoid the occasional mildew causing mid-summer rainstorm, a cabbage moth, or an ant invasion. Which are bound to happen eventually.

So to avoid most issues before they become problems, you have to be paying attention to your garden and giving it the love and support it requires.

This may mean paying attention to the forecast, pruning your plants when they need it, and keeping weeds to a minimum. With little effort, you can grow a bountiful organic garden of fresh fruit and vegetables by just being proactive and paying attention regularly to your garden and its needs.

Note: Ladybugs are an inexpensive, natural pest control solution since they feed on other insects to survive. They also won't hurt people, plants or pets.

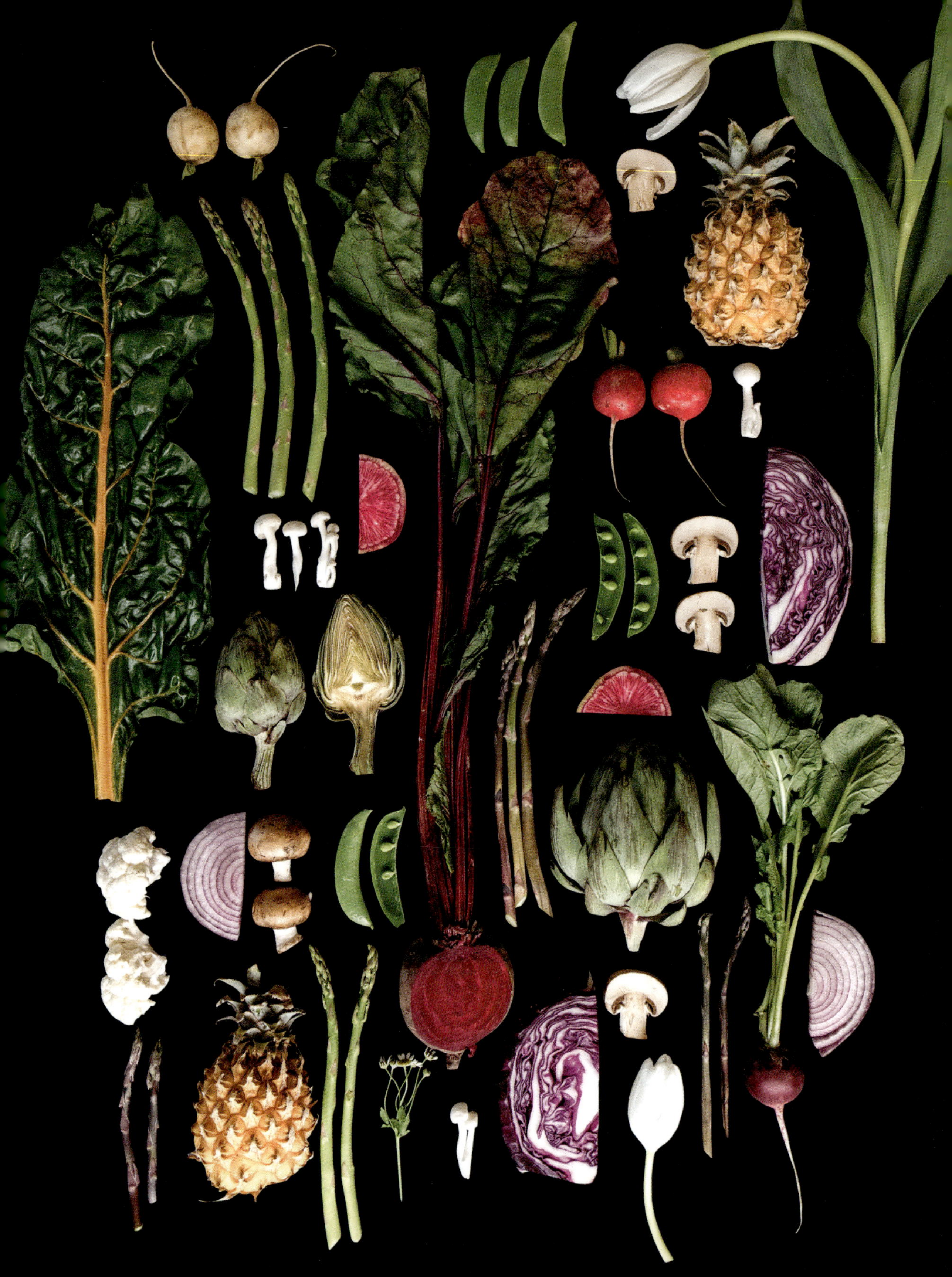

Spring

When I was a kid, I wasn't particularly fond of beets. To me, beets were more a form of punishment than enjoyment. They were fleshy, smelly, and came from a can. I never understood why anyone would eat them.

But now I have such a love for beets, and I enjoy them most in Spring. I often juice with them, I pickle them, and my daughter and I love to make beet chips together, which is one of her favorite snacks.

Beets and other spring fruits and vegetables all have a commonality. They're healing in that they help the body recover and rejuvenate from the long season of winter.

So put the coats and fleece–lined boots away, grab your Truvani reusable cooler bag, and I'll see you at the Farmer's Market. Together, let's grab as much asparagus and spring peas as we can carry and make something wonderful!

Xo,
Vani

MARCH
what's in season

Endive  Fennel  Spring Onions

Radishes  Lettuce  Cauliflower

Spinach  Pineapple  Mushrooms  Artichoke

16 | EAT SEASONALLY

APRIL
what's in season

Pineapple  Mushrooms  Avocado

Spring Peas  Lettuce Greens  Asparagus

Radishes  Rhubarb  Artichoke  Beets

MAY
what's in season

Asparagus	Strawberries	Apricots
Brussels Sprouts	Peas	Radishes
Mushrooms	Avocado	Artichoke	Kale

Seasonal Spotlights

Artichokes

HAVE YOU EVER NOTICED HOW CLEAN YOUR MOUTH FEELS AFTER ENJOYING AN ARTICHOKE?

If so, then it may not surprise you to learn that in ancient Greece, artichokes were used both as a breath freshener and as a deodorant.

This is because artichokes are a natural detoxifier.

But freshening your breath and detoxifying your body is just the tip of the iceberg in terms of why artichokes are good for you. In fact, artichokes rank among the top 10 most antioxidant-rich foods you can eat and boast a wide variety of benefits.

This is because in addition to antioxidants, artichokes also contain quite a bit of protein, are a great source of folate, fiber, prebiotics, and a wide spectrum of vitamins, including C, K, and all the B6 and B12. They are also a great source of a variety of minerals like calcium, iron, zinc, potassium, manganese, sodium, and phosphorus.

So whether you're looking to boost your immune system, improve your cardiovascular health, or nurture a healthy gut-microbiome, enjoying artichokes from April through June is a great way to eat seasonally and healthfully.

One of our favorite ways to enjoy artichokes is grilling them on the BBQ.

Note:

To ensure perfectly grilled artichokes, steam them until fully cooked before placing halves (face down) on an oiled grill. Then you cook them for a few additional minutes until grill lines appear and finish off with coarse sea salt, ground pepper, and fresh lemon.

Asparagus

WHETHER EATEN RAW, GRILLED, OR SAUTEED, FRESH GARDEN ASPARAGUS IS ARGUABLY ONE OF THE BEST THINGS ABOUT THE SPRING!

This is good because asparagus is nutritious and can help improve your health in a variety of ways.

If you're trying to lose weight or maintain a healthy weight, asparagus can help since it naturally reduces water weight and bloat. But that's not where the benefits of asparagus ends.

Known to be beneficial for eye health and to helpful in boosting mood, asparagus also helps detoxify the body and is excellent for urinary tract health. This is because asparagus is high in the amino acid asparagine, which helps flush the body of excess salt and toxins.

While the most common type of asparagus found in the market are the green varieties, there are also purple and white varieties of asparagus. You're more likely to find these gems at your local farmer's market and at local produce stands.

All asparagus varieties - even the white varieties - are high in antioxidants (especially vitamin E), but the purple varieties are especially so. Purple asparagus are loaded with anthocyanins, an antioxidant that helps prevent cancer since it attacks damaging free radicals in the body.

Note:

When trimming asparagus stalks, save the ends and store in the freezer to use later in casseroles, quiche, and soups. They're also ideal for making tasty sauces or smoothies.

Beets

YOU'VE PROBABLY HEARD THE ADVICE THAT THE MORE COLORFUL YOUR FRUITS AND VEGETABLES ARE, THE HEALTHIER THEY ARE.

This is because vibrant color in your produce is a signal that it contains a lot of healthy antioxidants.

Beets are no exception to this with the deep color of beets coming from the betalain pigment.

This pigment is loaded with phytochemical compounds like glycine, anthocyanins, carotenoids, lutein/zeaxanthin, and betaine. It's also full of a variety of vitamins and minerals as well.

In addition to the betalain pigment, beets are also high in fiber and are low in calories and fat.

So what do all these phytochemical compounds, vitamins, minerals and fiber do for the body?

Beets are great at helping fight inflammation, lowering blood pressure, aiding digestion, boosting brain and liver health, and fighting cancer.

Add to that the energy boost that beets provide from being high in complex carbohydrates, and the fact that they are available almost year-round, and beets could be considered a superfood!

Note:

When cutting greens off of beets, leave at least 1 to 2 inches of stem and do not trim root ends. This will help to keep the beets from bleeding.

Strawberries

THERE ARE NOT MANY THINGS IN THIS WORLD AS DELICIOUS AS FRESH, PERFECTLY RIPE STRAWBERRIES.

Add to that the numerous health benefits of strawberries, and you've got one of Mother Nature's little perfections.

Strawberries come into season in the Spring, and depending on the growing region can be enjoyed fresh through the beginning of Summer. Best to stock up and enjoy this sweet fruit as much as you can because your whole body will thank you.

According to a study, women who consumed three or more servings a week of strawberries decreased their risk of heart attack by 34%. This is because strawberries are full of antioxidants like anthocyanins that relax the blood vessels, which helps lower blood pressure.

Also, strawberries are loaded with fiber, vitamins, and folate, all of which contribute to a healthy heart and lower cholesterol levels.

The high vitamin count and variety of antioxidants in strawberries also help fight inflammation, which can help prevent stroke and a variety of diseases, including cancer.

Strawberries are also a great source of iodine, which is essential for a healthy thyroid and brain.

Note:

If you like to add fresh kale and spinach into your smoothies, consider strawberry tops an extra dose of greens. Instead of cutting off the top, drop the whole strawberry in the blender.

Ingredients Matter

THE STAR OF OUR POWDERS IS ORGANIC PEA PROTEIN.

When we were creating our protein powder, we tested sources for pea protein for MONTHS....and almost scrapped the product altogether.

We contacted 52 separate sources for the ingredients in our protein powder. Most of them failed our initial questioning, and the few that passed our initial questions sent over a sample for testing... and each source failed the heavy metals test.

Then, we stumbled on one unique source of organic pea protein. They did things slightly differently. Instead of turning a complete pea—pod and all—into pea protein, they would de-pod the peas first, and turn just the peas into pea protein.

And this source worked. Thankfully.

At Truvani, if we can't get ingredients to pass our standards we don't make the product.

Our Chocolate Plant Based Protein Powder has only 6 Ingredients

Our Vanilla Protein Powder has just 5 Ingredients

24 | EAT SEASONALLY

Spring Recipes

TRUVANI'S

Protein Waffles

1 SCOOP TRUVANI VANILLA OR CHOCOLATE PROTEIN POWDER

½ CUP BROWN RICE (OR OAT) FLOUR

¾ CUP WATER

1 TSP BAKING POWDER

2 EGGS

MIXED NUTS (OPTIONAL)

SLICED STRAWBERRIES, PINEAPPLE, OR APRICOTS (OPTIONAL SEASONAL FRUIT)

RECIPE DESCRIPTION:

If you want to know the secret to moist, delicious waffles that the whole family will devour without asking for syrup, it's to add in fresh fruit to the batter before cooking. Many are familiar with adding bananas, but any seasonal fruit will do!

RECIPE INSTRUCTIONS:

Mix all ingredients into a bowl and cook as directed using a waffle iron.

Top with mixed nuts and additional fresh fruit.

RECIPE INSPIRATION:

Many on the Truvani team have young families, and feeding our littles a nutritious and healthy breakfast is super important. We love this waffle recipe because it uses our Truvani Protein Powder, is quick, and doesn't include added sugar.

JM MAXWELL'S

Holy Kale Chocolate Smoothie

1 SCOOP TRUVANI CHOCOLATE PROTEIN POWDER

1-2 CUPS ORGANIC SPRING KALE

1 ½ CUPS ORGANIC ALMOND MILK UNSWEETENED VANILLA FLAVOR (OR BEVERAGE OF YOUR CHOICE)

¼ CUP WALNUTS & ALMONDS MIXED

¼ CUP BLACKBERRIES AND BLUEBERRIES (OR SEASONAL FRUIT)

RECIPE PROVIDED BY JM MAXWELL

RECIPE DESCRIPTION:

A delicious organic spring mix of fresh greens, berry fruit, nuts, and Truvani Chocolate Protein Powder. Also included? A whole lotta love! Serves 1.

RECIPE INSTRUCTIONS:

With a grateful heart, combine all ingredients with Truvani Chocolate Protein Powder in blender until smooth. While you wait for your delicious masterpiece, go ahead and find your happy place. Sing, dance, or play some upbeat music, and before you know it you'll be enjoying your Holy Kale Chocolate Smoothie!

Cheers & Much Love, JM

> " Inspiration for this recipe came from my desire for a breakfast smoothie that is all the things: Healthy, Easy Peasy & Super Delicious. "
>
> JM MAXWELL

TRUVANI'S
Beet & Avocado Salad with Orange Maple Vinaigrette

Salad

- 6 BEETS, WASHED AND TRIMMED
- 1 AVOCADO, HALVED AND DICED 
- 2 TBSP OLIVE OIL 
- SALT AND PEPPER 

Dressing

- ¼ CUP APPLE CIDER VINEGAR
- ¼ CUP ORANGE JUICE, FRESHLY SQUEEZED 
- ¼ CUP OLIVE OIL 
- 1 SCOOP TRUVANI MARINE COLLAGEN POWDER 
- ½ SHALLOT, MINCED 
- 1 TSP CINNAMON 
- 2 TBSP MAPLE SYRUP 
- 1 TBSP DIJON MUSTARD 
- ½ TSP SEA SALT

RECIPE DESCRIPTION:

Pair with your favorite grilled protein and quinoa for a quick and easy dinner. Serves 4.

RECIPE INSTRUCTIONS:

Preheat the oven to 450°. Place the beets on a sheet pan and roast until tender (around 1 hour). Let cool and then cut into cubes.

For dressing, shake all ingredients together in a mason jar, or mix in a blender until emulsified.

Add beets to a bowl with diced avocado, add dressing and mix until evenly coated.

KEANI GENZEL'S

Spring Strawberry Compote Stacker

1 LB FRESH STRAWBERRIES

3 TBS FRESH MINT, THINLY SLICED

1 SCOOP TRUVANI MARINE COLLAGEN POWDER

2 TBS HONEY (OR MAPLE SYRUP)

1 LEMON FOR JUICE AND ZEST

2 CUPS RAW ALMONDS

32 | EAT SEASONALLY

RECIPE PROVIDED BY KEANI GENZEL

RECIPE DESCRIPTION:

This is a fun and healthy clean eating snack that is "stacked" on rice cakes (or toast, English muffins, etc). They are super easy to make and look and taste fabulous! Store-bought almond butter may be used instead of homemade. The fruit compote is not technically a compote as is it is not heated but rather a "mixture".

RECIPE INSTRUCTIONS:

Chop or slice strawberries to your preference. Then combine strawberries, lemon juice, zest, mint, and honey in a bowl and lightly mix. Let sit in the refrigerator for 20 minutes (will keep in the fridge for 5-7 days).

For the almond butter, roast raw almonds in the oven at 350° for 10-15 minutes. Keep an eye on them so they don't burn. When the almonds are cool, put them in a food processor or blender and blend until creamy. Be patient with this process and be sure to let your food processor or blender cool down if it starts to get hot. The process of blending should take at least 15-20 minutes.

Spread some almond butter on a gluten-free rice cake or whichever base layer you would like to use. Layer some of the strawberry mixture over the almond butter. Add a topping if you would like such as coconut flakes or toasted almond slivers. Enjoy!

> " I own and operate a women's weekend yoga retreat and I am often the chef as well. I have fun with creating healthy and creative menus for the retreats. I enjoy the challenge of creating seasonal healthy meals and snacks that are interesting for the guests. They are often taken aback and surprised at how yummy clean eating can be.
>
> KEANI GENZEL "

TRUVANI'S

Grilled Artichokes with Lemon Garlic Dip

2 ARTICHOKES

1 CLOVE OF GARLIC, MINCED

1 TBSP DIJON MUSTARD

3 TBSP AVOCADO MAYONNAISE OR ORGANIC GREEK YOGURT

2 TBSP FRESHLY SQUEEZED LEMON JUICE

1 TSP SEA SALT

RECIPE DESCRIPTION:

A clean eating indulgent dip for spring! Instead of grilling, you could steam artichokes in an instant pot. Serves 2.

RECIPE INSTRUCTIONS:

Cut an inch off the stem of each artichoke. Place the artichokes, stem side up, in a steamer basket. Steam for about an hour (until base is tender).

Remove and let cool. Then slice in half and place face down on a hot grill until grill marks appear (approximately 3 minutes).

For the sauce, combine all ingredients in a small bowl and serve with the artichokes.

TRUVANI'S

Asparagus Soup

2 LBS FRESH ASPARAGUS, CHOPPED WITH ENDS TRIMMED

2 CLOVES GARLIC, CHOPPED

1 YELLOW ONION

4 TABLESPOONS OLIVE OIL

3 ½ CUPS CHICKEN OR VEGETABLE BROTH

1 CAN COCONUT MILK (FULL FAT OR LITE)

1 SCOOP TRUVANI MARINE COLLAGEN POWDER

1 TEASPOON FRESH ROSEMARY, CHOPPED

JUICE AND ZEST OF 1 LEMON

SEA SALT AND PEPPER TO TASTE

1 TABLESPOON FLAT LEAF PARSLEY, CHOPPED

RECIPE DESCRIPTION:

This soup can be enjoyed warm on a cool spring night, or cold when the sun is beaming and the weather is warm, or on a picnic under a blooming tree. Serves 4.

RECIPE INSTRUCTIONS:

In a large pot add olive oil and onion. Cook on medium heat until translucent (about 5 minutes).

Add garlic and sauté for about 2 minutes or until fragrant.

Add the asparagus and cook for another 5 minutes, then add the broth, coconut milk, Truvani Marine Collagen Powder and herbs. Cover and cook for 10 more minutes (or until asparagus is tender).

Turn off heat, add lemon juice. Transfer to either a food processor or blender. Blend on high. Serve either hot or cold.

YOORI KOO'S

Spring Pea Pasta

1 CUP DRY
CHICKPEA PASTA

½ CUP CASHEWS
(SOAKED FOR
A FEW HOURS)

4 TBSP
OLIVE OIL

2 TBSP
TRUVANI MARINE
COLLAGEN POWDER

JUICE OF ½ LEMON

1 STEM CURLY KALE,
FINELY CHOPPED

¼ CUP WATER

1 CUP FRESH
SPRING PEAS

1 CLOVE GARLIC,
MINCED

½ TSP
SEA SALT

½ TBSP
PINE NUTS

38 | EAT SEASONALLY

RECIPE PROVIDED BY YOORI KOO

RECIPE DESCRIPTION:

Gluten free pasta with pea lemon sauce and Truvani Marine Collagen Powder. Serves 2-4.

RECIPE INSTRUCTIONS:

Cook chickpea pasta to package instructions. Drain and keep aside. Put cashews, 3 tablespoons olive oil, Truvani Marine Collagen Powder, lemon juice, water and salt into a food processor and blend until smooth. Heat a medium sized pan with the remaining 1 tablespoon of olive oil. Finely grate garlic and add to the pan and cook until golden brown. Add peas and cook for about 5 minutes, then add kale. Take about 2/3 of the pea and kale mixture and add to the cashew sauce. Blend again until smooth and green. Add both the cashew sauce and pasta into the pan with the reamining peas and kale, toss until everything is evenly coated. Serve with pine nuts and enjoy while still warm!

RECIPE INSPIRATION:

Since I was 18 years old I have been obsessed with a healthy lifestyle. I was on a quest to find my own personal health. Extensive hours of researching the best products and foods to eat eventually led to me completing a certificate as an Integrative Nutrition Health Coach. Health to me means following a whole foods diet as much as possible and supplementing where needed.

> " Spring is my favorite time of year...with the anticipation of summer in the air it's time for lighter meals. This pasta dish is filling yet has a light and refreshing lemon tang - I prefer it warm, but it is also makes a great pasta salad to take on a picnic or to work!
>
> YOORI KOO "

PORSCHE LACEWELL'S

Spicy Breaded Cauliflower Spinach Fajitas

Breaded Cauliflower

1 HEAD CAULIFLOWER

1 CUP ROLLED OATS, CHOPPED

½ CUP ALMOND BUTTER

1 TSP CAYENNE PEPPER
1 TSP PAPRIKA
1 TSP GROUND PEPPER
1 TSP SALT

HONEY

Cilantro Sauce

1 BUNCH CILANTRO

1 AVOCADO

2 TBSP OLIVE OIL

2 TSP LIME JUICE

1 TSP SEA SALT

Spinach tortilla

1 CUP SPELT FLOUR

1 HANDFUL OF SPINACH

½ CUP WATER

2 TSP SEA SALT

RECIPE PROVIDED BY PORSCHE LACEWELL

RECIPE INSTRUCTIONS:

Breaded Cauliflower

Mix the spices and chopped oats in a small bowl, then stir in the almond butter and honey. Chop the cauliflower into bite-sized pieces and put in a large bowl. Pour mixture over the cauliflower and thoroughly mix until all pieces are covered. Bake the cauliflower on a cookie sheet for 20 minutes on 400° or until crisp.

Cilantro Sauce

Put the cilantro leaves, avocado (peeled and seeded), oil, fresh lime juice, and salt in blender. Blend until smooth.

Spinach Tortilla

In a food processor, add spinach, spelt flour, salt, and water and blend until dough forms. Remove and roll dough into medium sized balls with hand. Flatten with a rolling pin. Bake on a cookie sheet on 400° for 10 minutes. Let cool before adding the baked cauliflower. Top the fajita with the cilantro sauce and voila!

> "I had fajitas with my family and remembered a delicious Food Babe cauliflower popcorn recipe. I used to make it all the time. I thought the cilantro sauce would add a nice Spring touch to it and the spinach tortilla would make it that much healthier."
>
> PORSCHE LACEWELL

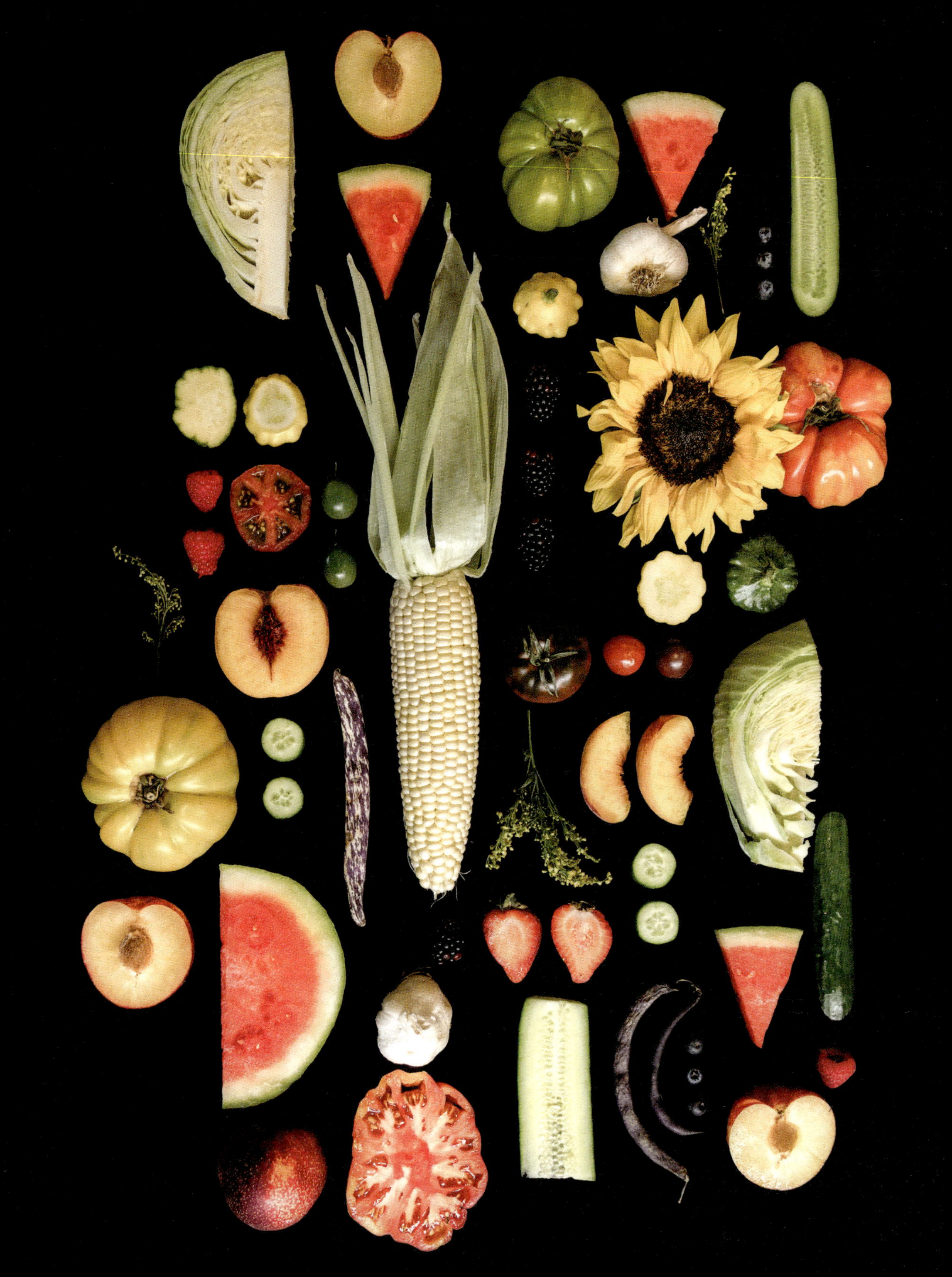

Summer

On a recent summer trip to Italy, I was served one of the most delicious desserts I can ever remember having. It wasn't tiramisu or gelato, it was watermelon.

Fresh slices of watermelon on the rind were served to us on a platter and garnished with thin ribbons of mint.

The watermelon, loaded with seeds, was bursting with flavor and was so so juicy. If there was an eating contest, I would've easily won. I devoured as much as could.

Watermelon represents everything I love about the summer bounty. Full of water, it helps keep the body hydrated - just like cucumbers, tomatoes, other melons, and berries.

Which reminds me of another favorite summer treat - blueberry muffins. If you've ever taken a bite of a freshly baked blueberry muffin—made with fresh blueberries—then you likely know what I mean. There are few things as delightful in this world as biting into a fresh-baked muffin and experiencing the pop of a warm baked blueberry.

Xo,
Vani

JUNE
what's in season

Garlic	Cherries	Cucumber
Kale	Strawberries	Cabbage
Carrots	Onion	Leek	Peas

44 | EAT SEASONALLY

JULY
what's in season

Strawberries	Zucchini	Corn
Cucumber	Cherries	Broccoli
Fennel	Apricots	Blueberries	Potatoes

AUGUST
what's in season

Zucchini	Peach	Tomatoes
Cauliflower	Cucumber	Green Beans
Peppers	Cantaloupe	Apples	Watermelons

46 | EAT SEASONALLY

Seasonal Spotlights

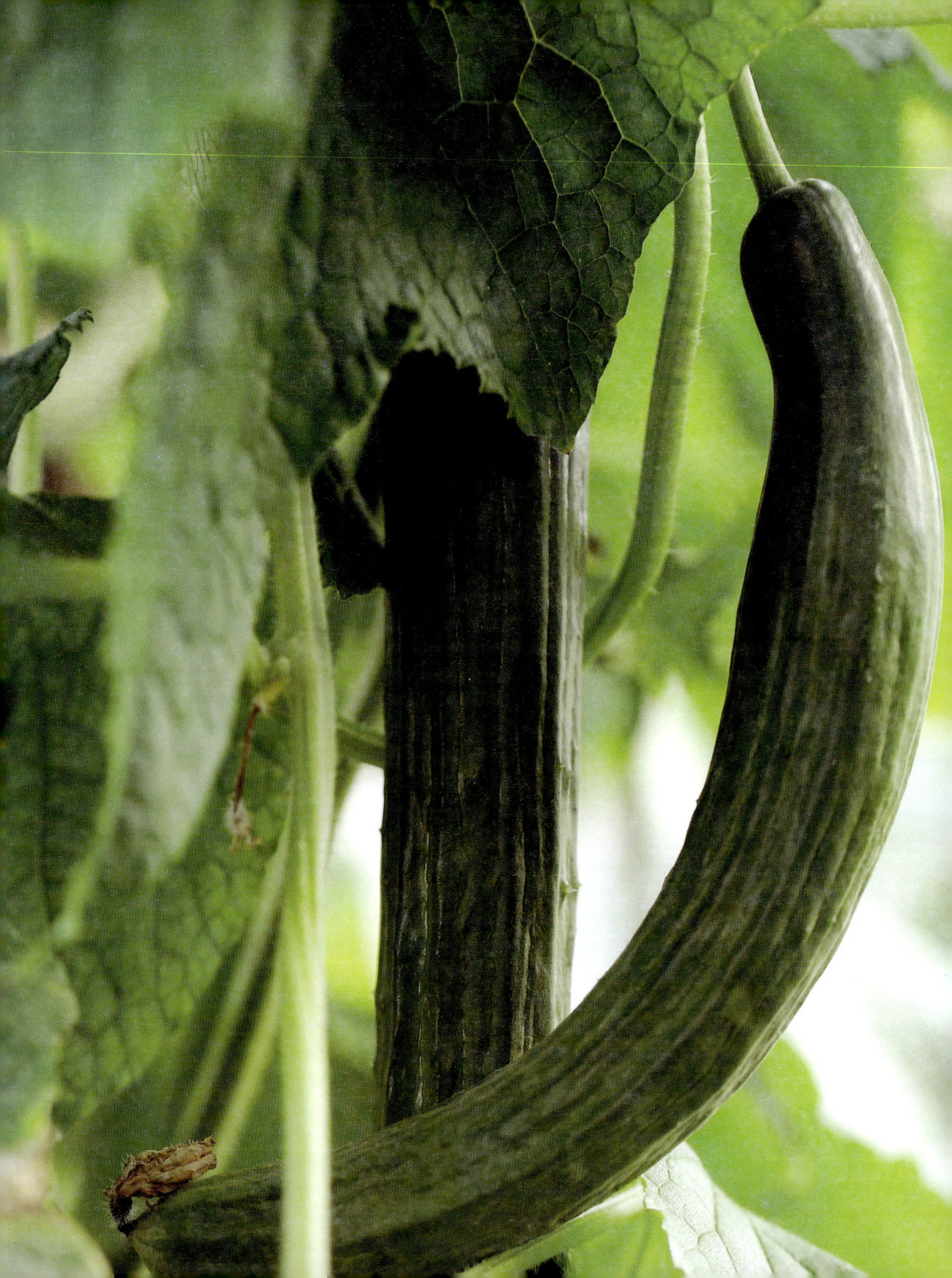

Cucumbers

THE VOTE IS IN. ONE OF THE MOST SATISFYING THINGS TO GROW IN A VEGETABLE GARDEN IS CUCUMBER.

That's because the cucumber is an easy grower and is such a giver. The more cucumbers you pick from your plant, the more cucumbers the plant produces!

Which is just fine with us. During the summer, when the weather is hot and the days are long, cucumbers come to the rescue.

Cucumbers are incredibly hydrating and are also impressively high in phytonutrients. In fact, research has identified 73 different compounds in cucumbers that provide us with antioxidant and anti-inflammatory benefits, which are key to our ability to fight disease.

But here's the kicker. Many of these compounds are found in the skin and seeds of the cucumber. So it's best to eat all parts if you can.

This is why growing your own cucumbers or shopping at a farmer's market is ideal.

To help keep cucumbers fresh longer, store–bought cucumbers tend to have a wax coating applied to the skin, which you then need to peel before eating.

No one wants to eat wax!

Note:

Try to pick cucumbers when they are of mature size. For slicing cucumber varieties, a mature fruit is around 6 to 8 inches. Pickling cucumbers mature fully around 3 to 4 inches.

Cantaloupes

SOMETIMES WE FORGET JUST HOW MARVELOUS A MELON THE CANTALOUPE IS!

Its pastel power is sometimes overlooked in contrast to more vibrantly colored fruits, but a cantaloupe's nutrient content is actually quite impressive.

Research shows that the beta-carotene content of a cantaloupe is about 30 times higher than that of an orange! The combination of beta-carotene and alpha-carotene—and other lesser-known carotenoid phytonutrients and cucurbitacins—in cantaloupe provides an anti-inflammatory armor for our bodies.

The cantaloupe also contains a good host of B vitamins, vitamin K, vitamin C, potassium, magnesium, copper, and fiber. Even the seeds of the cantaloupe are edible and provide a measurable amount of omega-3!

Like other melon, cantaloupe has a high water content that can help you stay hydrated amidst the summer heat. Because of this, cantaloupe may help prevent bloating and constipation (which is always a plus for our "systems" in any season).

Let's give this super melon some more table time this summer and mix it into our healthy lifestyles.

Note:

The easiest way to select the perfect cantaloupe is to pick it up and feel its weight. If it feels fuller and heavier than you'd expect, then that is a good indication that it is at its ideal ripeness. You can also smell the blossom end of the melon; the sweeter the aroma, the better. That means it's ready to eat.

Blueberries

THINK ABOUT CHILDREN GROWING UP THESE DAYS.

They are being raised in a world where Alexa is not a childhood friend, but a device they speak to that seemingly delivers groceries and convenience within the hour.

In today's world, it's not enough to teach our kids about where their food comes from, we must show them!

That's why on everyone's summer to-do list should be at least one visit to a pick-your-own blueberry farm.

Here your littles will be able to experience childlike wonder in the form of plump all-you-can-eat goodness.

Let them pick as much as they want and bring the bounty home. These sweet summer treats are not just tasty, but they are also packed with antioxidants called anthocyanins. Anthocyanins fight cell damage and reduce inflammation in the body.

Blueberries actually rank the highest of any fruit for antioxidants, so add them to salads, bake with them, add them by the handfuls to your smoothies, and enjoy!

Note:

Blueberries are among the most nutrient-dense berries. They are also about 85% water, and low in calories.

Ingredients Matter

IT'S IMPORTANT TO KNOW WHERE YOUR FRUITS AND VEGETABLES ARE FROM, AND HOW THEY WERE GROWN.

It's also very important to know where the ingredients in your supplements are from, and what else is put into your powders and pills.

At Truvani, we believe that when it comes to labels, LESS is more. That's why we avoid putting preservatives and useless additives into our products.

There are no natural or artificial flavors added to our powder, so you can enjoy it in everything from your coffee to a cool summer soup.

We love making smoothies with summer's amazing assortment of produce and adding in a scoop of collagen for an extra beauty boost.

Our Truvani collagen is sustainably sourced from WILD CAUGHT fish from the cold Northern waters off of Iceland and France.

We say NO to fish farms, and only buy from high quality sources.

Summer Recipes

ANGELA REUTTER'S

Power Up Banana Pancakes

1 RIPE BANANA

HANDFUL OF WALNUTS, CHOPPED

1 EGG

1 SCOOP TRUVANI VANILLA PLANT BASED PROTEIN POWDER

SPLASH OF MILK

DASH OF CINNAMON

BUTTER OR OIL TO GREASE PAN

MAPLE SYRUP

RECIPE PROVIDED BY ANGELA REUTTER

RECIPE DESCRIPTION:

These Power Up Banana Pancakes are unique because you can switch up the flavor. Some of my favorite ways to do that are by adding pumpkin pie spice, topping it with blueberries or even dark chocolate chips!

RECIPE INSTRUCTIONS:

Smash 1 ripe banana in a medium-sized bowl. Add in 1 scoop of Truvani Vanilla Protein Powder and mix together well. Add a splash of milk, 1 egg, and a dash of cinnamon, and whisk lightly. Heat an oiled pan (I prefer avocado oil) over medium heat. Once the pan is hot, pour about 1/3 of the batter into the pan, making a circle shape. Cook pancakes on each side for about 2-3 minutes or until desired thickness is reached. Continue to do the same with the rest of the batter. You should end up with 2-3 pancakes depending on your desired size. Top your delicious Power Up Banana Pancakes with chopped walnuts and organic maple syrup.

> My name is Angela Reutter and I truly believe that healthy eating is easier than it seems. I love experimenting in the kitchen and creating new unique recipes that satisfy my cravings! This is why I created the Power Up Banana Pancakes, to fuel your body with simple ingredients.
>
> ANGELA REUTTER

DEVRA STRUZENBERG'S

Vegan Vanilla Tropical Smoothie

¼ CUP PINEAPPLE, FRESH OR FROZEN

½ CUP STRAWBERRIES

1 SCOOP TRUVANI VANILLA PROTEIN POWDER

1 BANANA

¼ CUP MANGO

1 CUP ALMOND MILK, UNSWEETENED VANILLA FLAVOR

RECIPE PROVIDED BY DEVRA STRUZENBERG

RECIPE DESCRIPTION:

A refreshing fruit smoothie with Truvani Vanilla Protein Powder.

RECIPE INSTRUCTIONS:

Mix all ingredients in a blender to desired consistency. Add more almond milk (or water) to make the smoothie thinner or less to thicken. Freezing the fruit ahead of time makes this a quick and healthy breakfast or snack.

> " We like to make smoothies in our household. This one evolved this summer when we couldn't get enough mango and were rushing to summer camp and work every morning!
>
> DEVRA STRUZENBERG "

ALISON HITE'S

Bad B Smoothie

2 LARGE CARROTS

½ BANANA

½ AVOCADO

1 SCOOP TRUVANI PROTEIN POWDER

1 CUP BERRIES

1 TBSP ALMOND BUTTER

1 CUP CASHEW YOGURT

HANDFUL OF GREENS

1 TSP ASHWAGANDHA ROOT

1 TSP BEE POLLEN

½ CUP FLAX SEEDS

1 TRUVANI TURMERIC TABLET

COCONUT WATER TO THE TOP

2 ICE CUBES

DASH OF CINNAMON

RECIPE PROVIDED BY ALISON HITE

RECIPE DESCRIPTION:

A meal replacement smoothie, packed with plant power!

RECIPE INSTRUCTIONS:

Blend all ingredients in a blender to desired consistency.

INSPIRATION FOR RECIPE:

I'm Alison from @thecheekyclean. When I committed to living an organic, nutritious, and CLEAN lifestyle, the first daily change I made was to improve my eating habits. I replaced a toxin-filled "to go" lunch or breakfast on the road into a nutritious, delicious, easy smoothie. The cheeky name has just stuck with my community, and I love seeing all the Bad B Smoothie photos that my tribe posts! Until Truvani created a protein powder, I could not find anything on the market clean enough to be approved or recommended for use in my smoothie as a meal.

> This smoothie is packed with beneficial ingredients for the body and keeps me strong & focused daily.
>
> ALISON HITE

TRUVANI'S

Strawberry Salad with Salmon with Collagen Rich Balsamic Dressing

Salad

- ½ QUART FRESH STRAWBERRIES, SLICED
- ½ LB FRESH BABY SPINACH 
- ¼ RED ONION, THINLY SLICED 
- SLICED ALMONDS FOR TOPPING (OPTIONAL) 
- CRUMBLED GOAT CHEESE TO SPRINKLE ON TOP (OPTIONAL) 

Dressing

- ¼ CUP BALSAMIC VINEGAR
- ½ CUP EXTRA VIRGIN OLIVE OIL 
- ¼ CUP COCONUT SUGAR 
- 1 SCOOP TRUVANI MARINE COLLAGEN 
- 1 TBSP POPPY SEEDS 
- 1 TBSP RED ONION, MINCED 

Salmon

- 2-3 FILETS OF WILD CAUGHT SALMON
- AVOCADO OIL 
- LEMON JUICE 
- SALT AND PEPPER

RECIPE DESCRIPTION:

Do you know the special reason why spinach and strawberries go so well together? In addition to being a delicious combination, the vitamin C from the strawberries helps your body better absorb the iron from the spinach! Add a grilled wild caught salmon filet to the salad and you have one power house of nutrition to enjoy this summer!

RECIPE INSTRUCTIONS:

Prepare and heat grill. Oil salmon filets and season with salt and pepper. Grill until desired doneness.

For the dressing, mix all ingredients in a mason jar and/or container with sealable lid. Shake until coconut sugar and Truvani Marine Collagen Powder dissolve or use an electric frother to mix all ingredients. Set aside.

For the salad, combine all ingredients into a bowl and right before serving, lightly dress salad with dressing and top with salmon filet.

KELLIE SHIRLEY'S

Gluten Free Pita/Naan Bread

1 ½ CUPS OF CASSAVA FLOUR

1 ¼ CUP FILTERED WATER

¼ CUP AVOCADO OIL OR EXTRA-VIRGIN OLIVE OIL

SALT AND PEPPER

½ TSP MELTED GHEE

1 SCOOP TRUVANI MARINE COLLAGEN POWDER

¼ TSP GARLIC POWDER

1 TBSP GROUNDED FLAX SEEDS (OPTIONAL)

RECIPE PROVIDED BY KELLIE SHIRLEY

RECIPE DESCRIPTION:

These little guys are great for a sandwich, appetizer or even an afternoon snack dipped in hummus or guacamole.

RECIPE INSTRUCTIONS:

In a large bowl, mix all ingredients together until a ball of soft dough forms.

Separate the dough into small pieces (might be a little sticky, but that's okay!) and place one by one onto either a grill pan or regular cast iron/frying pan. Flatten them out as much as you can.

Cook on a low-medium heat until both sides are brown, bubbly and crispy (takes about 5 minutes per side). Let sit for a few minutes to cool.

RECIPE INSPIRATION:

I have been following Food Babe for many years now and have been a HUGE supporter of her over the years. I remember learning about her back in college and doing her 7-Day Sugar Detox, which instantly lead me to discovering my passion for health and wellness. From all of her recipes, educational content and her new business, Truvani, I have learned SO much about the industry (and my health in general) and am so grateful for her dedication to her customers and mission! On my blog, one of my friends always messaged me asking to create a gluten-free naan bread. So naturally, it had to happen. Adding Truvani Marine Collagen Powder simply takes the recipe to the next level - a great way to get some added protein without even knowing it!

TEDDI VESEY'S

Spicy Black Bean Salsa

Salsa

2 CANS BLACK BEANS, DRAINED AND RINSED

1 CAN DICED, GREEN CHILIES

½ BUNCH CILANTRO

2 CLOVES GARLIC, MINCED

1 SMALL RED ONION, CHOPPED

1 JALAPENO, SEEDED AND DICED

Dressing

1-2 LIMES, JUICED

1-2 TBSPS OF DIJON MUSTARD

½ CUP OLIVE OIL

1 TSP CUMIN SEED

SALT TO TASTE

RECIPE PROVIDED BY TEDDI VESEY

RECIPE DESCRIPTION:

This salsa can be used as a topping on a salad, appetizer or toasted bread.

RECIPE INSTRUCTIONS:

Add all salsa and dressing ingredients in a bowl and stir until combined. Add salt to taste.

> " A friend of a friend of a friend served it at a gathering years ago. It was so delicious. I make it on a regular basis. "
>
> TEDDI VESEY

TRUVANI'S
Tomato Gazpacho

4 LARGE (OR 9 SMALL) VINE RIPE RED TOMATOES

1 CUCUMBER, PEELED AND SEEDED

1 MEDIUM BELL PEPPER, CORED AND SEEDED

1 SMALL SWEET YELLOW ONION, CUT INTO CHUNKS

¼ CUP HIGH QUALITY EXTRA-VIRGIN OLIVE OIL

1 LARGE GARLIC CLOVE, PEELED

¼ + CUP FRESH BASIL LEAVES, PLUS EXTRA FOR GARNISH

2 TABLESPOONS RED WINE VINEGAR

SEA SALT AND PEPPER TO TASTE

RECIPE DESCRIPTION:

This soup is an explosion of summer flavors, which is sure to delight anyone who loves picnics, long days at the beach, or BBQs with friends and family. Texture is important for this gazpacho, so process your ingredients in the blender at various stages to ensure a silky soup base. Serves 4.

RECIPE INSTRUCTIONS:

Before you add all your veggies to the blender, set aside about 1/2 cup of the juicy tomato core with seeds and about 1/4 of the cucumber and 1/4 of the bell pepper. These will be used as a garnish, so finely dice these veggies, add a pinch of salt, and store in the fridge until ready to serve.

Chop the remaining veggies into chunks. Put all of the onion into the blender and 1/2 of the chopped tomato, cucumber, and bell pepper. Then add the basil, olive oil, garlic, and salt and pepper. Start the blender at a slow speed and gradually increase the speed of this first portion until mixture is smooth.

Add the remaining tomato, cucumber, and bell pepper to the mixture and continue to blend until it reaches desired consistency. Some people love a really creamy gazpacho, and others like little chunks of veggies for texture. Remove from blender and chill for at least 2 hours before serving, or up to 24 hours.

Add salt and pepper to taste and garnish with finely diced tomato, cucumber, and bell pepper. For an added boost, stir in one scoop of Truvani Marine Collagen Powder to soup before serving.

MARY TERDICH'S

Sweet Potato Pattie Burgers

2 CANS
CANNELLINI BEANS

1 LARGE
SWEET POTATO

2 TBSP TAHINI

1 TSP CUMIN
¼ TSP GROUND PEPPER
DASH OF CAYENNE PEPPER
SALT TO TASTE

⅛ - ¼ CUP
OF NUTRITIONAL YEAST

¼ CUP FLOUR
OR GROUND ALMONDS

68 | EAT SEASONALLY

RECIPE PROVIDED BY MARY TERDICH

RECIPE DESCRIPTION:

Delicious and savory plant based burgers that are easy to make ahead. Even meat eaters love them! We tend to eat these burgers more in the summer, but they are great year round for lunch or dinner.

RECIPE INSTRUCTIONS:

Peel and slice sweet potato. Place on a lined baking sheet and spread in an even layer. Cook in oven until roasted. Remove and set aside to cool. Place sweet potato in a large bowl, add drained beans and smash together. Stir in reamining ingredients and any other desired seasonings. Sweet potato mixture should be soft and moist. If necessary, add more flour or ground almonds to thicken.

Heat 1 tablespoon of avocado oil in a large frying pan over medium-high heat. Form patties from the sweet potato mixture and coat thickly in ground almonds (or bread crumbs). Place in frying pan and cook untill golden brown on both sides.

Serve on a toasted bun with your favorite burger toppings.

Note: Yes this pattie does kind of fall apart as you eat it. But that's OK because it tastes so yummy!

> " I wanted to create something that was similar to a veggie burger I ate in a local restaurant. My entire family, even the meat lovers, love it! "
>
> MARY TERDICH

TRUVANI'S

Summer Bounty Bowl with Collagen Goddess Dressing

Salad

- 1 HANDFUL ARUGULA
- ¼ CUP RIPE CHERRY TOMATOES 
- ½ CUP QUINOA, COOKED
- ¼ CUP CHICKPEAS, ROASTED 
- ½ CUCUMBER, SLICED 
- ½ RED PEPPER, SLICED 
- ¼ ZUCCHINI, SLICED 

Dressing

- ¼ CUP TAHINI
- 3 TBSP WATER 
- 2 TBSP OLIVE OIL 
- 1 SCOOP TRUVANI MARINE COLLAGEN POWDER 
- ¼ CUP LEMON JUICE 
- 1 TSP SESAME OIL 
- 1 CLOVE GARLIC, MINCED 
- 1 TBSP FRESH DILL 
- 1 TBSP FRESH CHIVES
- 1 TBSP FRESH PARSLEY, FINELY CHOPPED
- 1 TBSP SOY SAUCE
- SALT AND PEPPER TO TASTE

RECIPE DESCRIPTION:

The beauty of making a bounty bowl is to use whatever ingredients are seasonal and at their peak of freshness and taste! Below is our summer inspired bounty bowl, which includes a mix of raw and roasted veggies, but feel free to substitute ingredients based on your garden harvest or farmer's market specials!

RECIPE INSTRUCTIONS:

Dressing

Add all ingredients to a deep bowl and whisk together until well blended. Add salt and pepper to taste. Store in the fridge in a sealed container for up to a week.

Bounty Bowl

Cook quinoa according to directions. Heat oven to 425°. Lightly toss sliced zucchini and bell pepper with olive oil. Spread out zucchini, bell pepper, and chickpeas on a lightly oiled baking pan. Salt and pepper contents of sheet pan and roast in the oven for 10-12 minutes until desired doneness. Set aside and let cool.

To arrange your bowl, first add greens (arugula) to the bottom of the bowl. Then start building. Add a scoop of quinoa to one side of the bowl, followed by a raw ingredient (tomatoes), followed by a roasted ingredient (zucchini). Alternate between roasted and raw ingredients in bowl until your bounty is overflowing! Drizzle with dressing and enjoy!

MARIANNA'S
Tomato Garlic Grillin' Sauce

VINE RIPE RED TOMATOES

GARLIC
(TO TASTE)

APPLE CIDER VINEGAR
(TO TASTE)

SALT

PEPPER

RECIPE PROVIDED BY MARIANNA

RECIPE DESCRIPTION:

No need for ketchup! This grillin' sauce will add a delightful zip to your summer BBQs, and can be canned or frozen for year-round use.

RECIPE INSTRUCTIONS:

Cut tomatoes in quarters. In a bowl add tomatoes, crushed garlic cloves (how many depends on your flavor preference), a splash of apple cider vinegar and salt and pepper. Blend ingredients together. Adjust salt, pepper and vinegar to taste. You can also add some sugar for a sweeter taste. Transfer the mixture to jars with lids and refrigerate. Use within a week or store in the freezer.

> " This family recipe came from my childhood living in Yakutsk (north Russia). We had long, cold winters and during those months we didn't have any fresh fruits or vegetables. My parents made this sauce in the summer and we had it year round as a delicious addition to many meals like hot dogs, dumplings, chicken, fish, etc.
>
> MARIANNA "

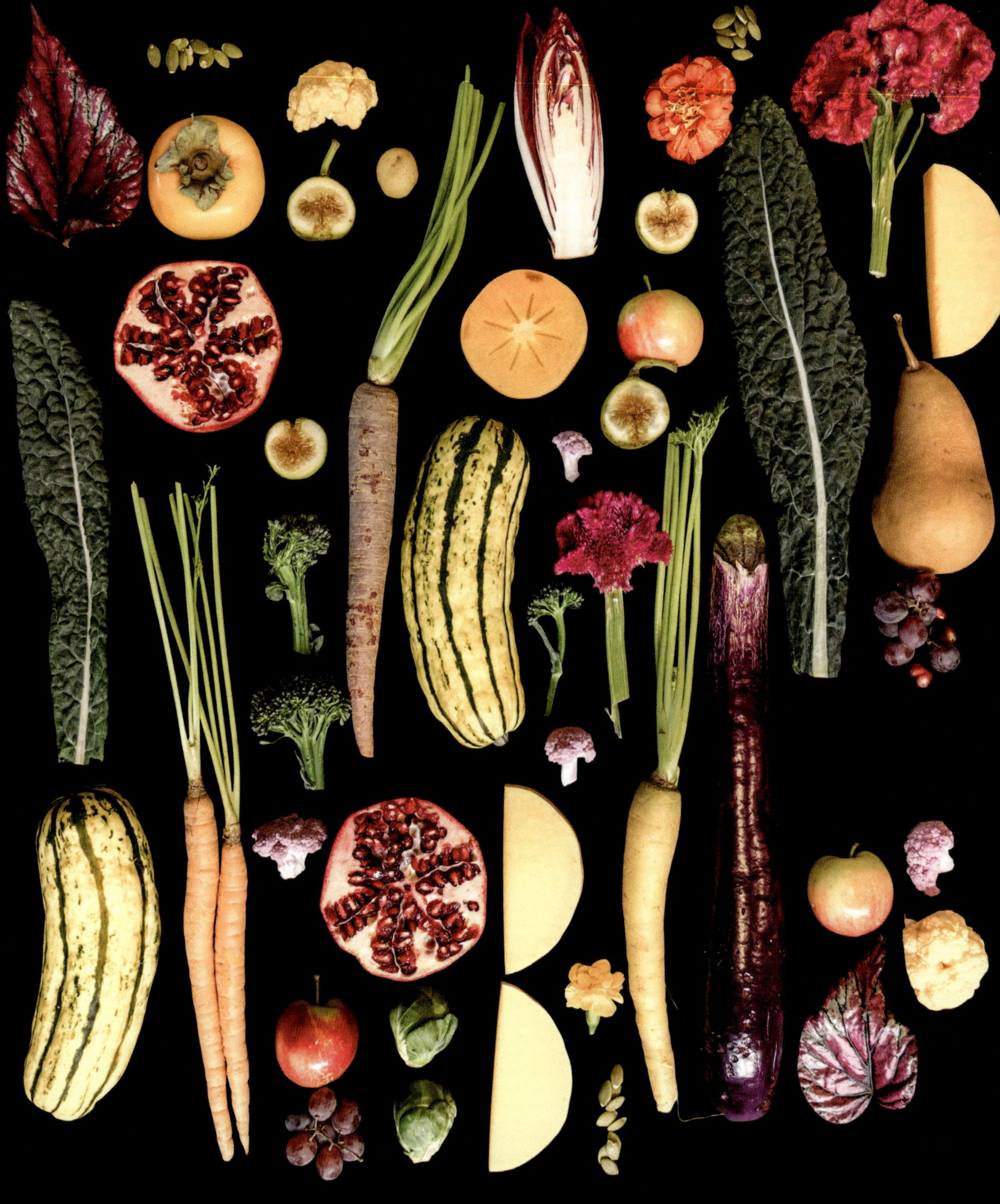

Fall

I used to travel to Michigan for work, and in the fall months I always did one thing before traveling back home. Before heading to the airport, I would stop by the local Farmer's Market and buy as many Honeycrisp apples as I could carry home.

Have you ever had a Honeycrisp apple? They are so good. Fresh Honeycrisp apples have the perfect crunch, are perfectly sweet, and are my favorite type of apple when I can find them ripe off the tree.

And they're ripe in the fall after spending their summer growing on the tree.

Where summer is full of berries, salads, and lots of barbeques, in the fall we start making the transition back to the kitchen to spend more time with the stove and oven. In this chapter, we're pleased to share a collection of fall-inspired recipes provided by friends of Truvani.

Enjoy!

Xo,
Vani

SEPTEMBER
what's in season

Squash

Cabbage

Tomatoes

Pomegranates

Pumpkins

Grapes

Kale

Persimmons

Pears

Peppers

OCTOBER
what's in season

Carrots	Cabbage	Tomatoes
Acorn Squash	Pumpkins	Eggplant
Kale	Cauliflower	Apples	Broccoli

EAT SEASONALLY

NOVEMBER
what's in season

Chard	Cabbage	Kale
Sweet Potatoes	Pumpkins	Brussels Sprouts
Cauliflower	Apples	Broccoli	Beets

Seasonal Spotlights

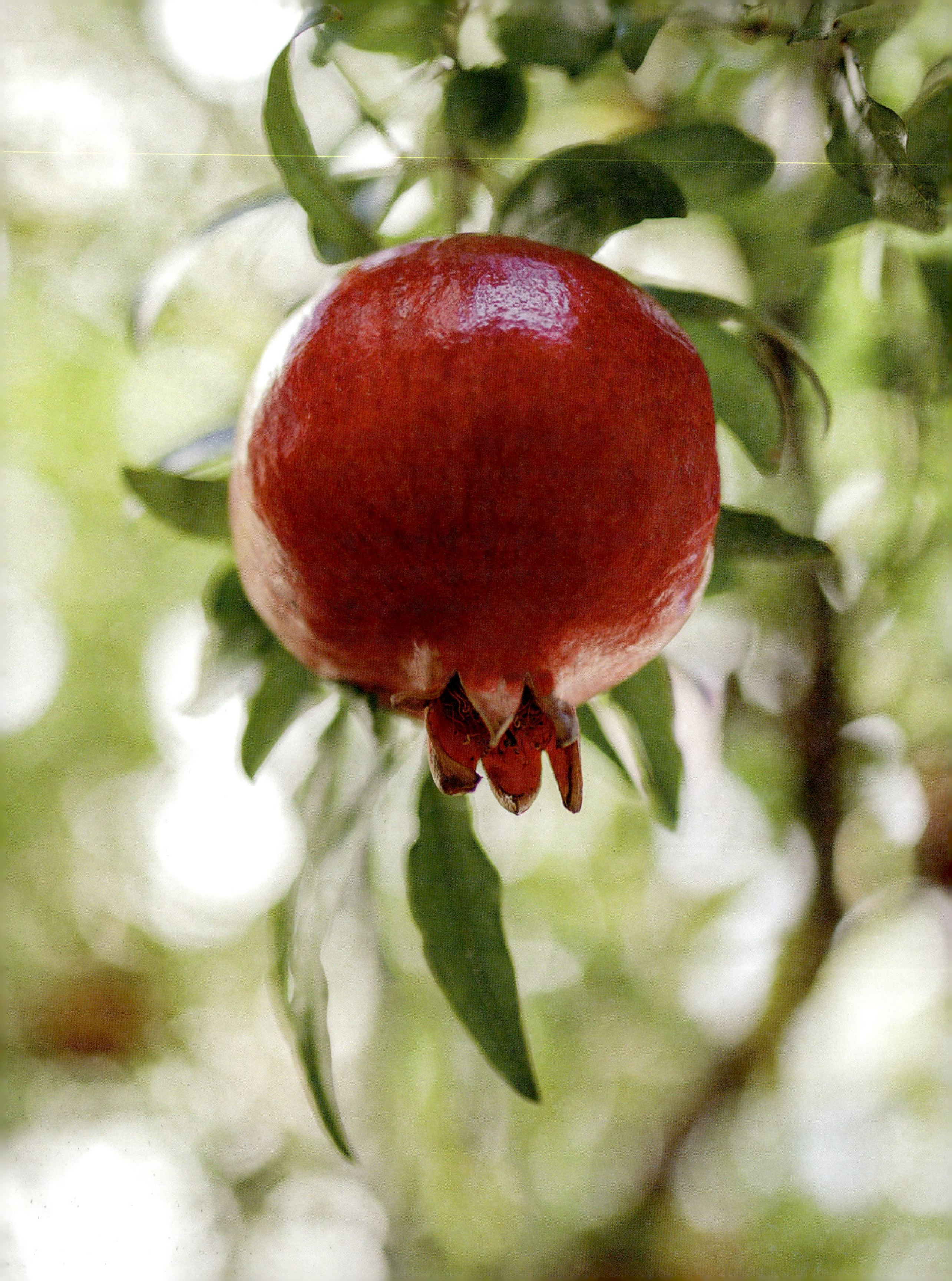

Pomegranates

THE POMEGRANATE IS THE PERFECT EXAMPLE OF A SEASONAL FRUIT. GREEK MYTHOLOGY CREDITS POMEGRANATES FOR THE CHANGING OF THE SEASONS.

The myth starts with Hades, the god of the Underworld, and Persephone, daughter of Zeus and Demeter, the goddess of harvest and fertility.

As the legend goes, Hades kidnapped Persephone one day so that she would become his wife in the Underworld.

Demeter, devastated by the loss of her daughter, went into mourning. As a result, all things ceased to grow on the earth as it fell into an eternal winter.

To keep her with him, Hades tricked Persephone into eating pomegranate seeds, the result of which is a doomed fate to live in the Underworld with him for eternity. But since she only ate six seeds, he only could compel her to stay six months of the year with him.

The other six months, she was free to return to Earth to be with her mother. When Persephone was able to be with her mother, for six months, things grew, and life flourished.

Perhaps this is why the pomegranate is such a tricky fruit to cut and eat? It represents the struggle that Persephone and her mother went through to be together.

But all that effort is certainly worth it!

Pomegranate seeds, which are called "arils," are loaded with nutritional value and are incredibly healthy.

Note:

Pomegranates are full of fiber and contain Punicic acid, (a conjugated linoleic acid) and punicalagins (an antioxidant). Both of these support lowering inflammation in the body and fighting disease.

Apples

HAVE YOU EVER BEEN BOBBING FOR APPLES?

This (once) popular children's Halloween game has its roots way back when the Romans invaded what is now Britain. The Romans brought the apple tree with them, which represented Pomona, the goddess of plenty.

The Celtic people started incorporating apples into their annual festivities and games. One game involved single people bobbing for apples. The first person to successfully grab an apple with their teeth would then be the first person allowed to marry.

With this knowledge, you may not want your pre-teen bobbing for apples anytime soon, but don't limit their access to this delicious and nutritious fruit!

Apples pack a lot of punch in the fiber department, so they're a great way to get a snack in, regulate energy, and curb appetite.

And they're also loaded with antioxidants, which is one of the many reasons they're so healthy. One antioxidant in particular, quercetin, works to boost our immune system.

In fact, apples may just be the perfect antidote to the stress our bodies go through when trying to adjust to the cooler weather and shorter days.

Note:

Apples are also loaded with **Vitamin C**, which makes this fruit particularly deserving of the saying "An apple a day keeps the doctor away."

Kale

KALE—OR LEAFY CABBAGE—IS A REMARKABLE MEMBER OF THE CRUCIFEROUS FAMILY.

Kale is known for its ability to thrive during the colder seasons of the year. In fact, kale actually becomes a bit sweeter after it goes through a frost!

Even though it's been a superfood for humans since before 2000 BC, Kale has recently become quite trendy.

And for a good reason.

High in fiber, those stems and leaves are a highly concentrated source of antioxidants and contain anti-inflammatory nutrients good for the whole body.

Look for kale with firm, deeply colored leaves and moist hardy stems.

Because kale is incredibly versatile, pick some up and get creative!

You could add chopped kale to your fall stews and soups for an added nutrient boost.

You can juice it or add it to your power smoothies.

You can shave it and add it to your favorite salad, frittata, or on pizza!

Note:

For a quick and easy side that the whole family will love, try sautéeing a bunch of kale with olive oil. Squeeze fresh lemon juice on top and add a dash of salt and pepper. Yum!

Ingredients Matter

FALL IS A FANTASTIC SEASON TO PULL OUT SOME OF YOUR FAVORITE SPICES.

Our organic Turmeric powder is available in a unique uncoated tablet that you can toss into soups, lattes, or even hot water to make simple turmeric tea.

This is in addition to simply taking our Turmeric as a daily supplement to help maintain healthy inflammation responses, promote overall joint mobility, and support brain, digestive, and heart health.

With added Black Pepper to help with absorbency, our Truvani Turmeric is USDA certified organic and non-GMO.

The warm taste of our Turmeric tablet blends beautifully into soups, stews, and sauces. When adding our Truvani Turmeric to your favorite dishes, we recommend using 3 tablets for every tablespoon of turmeric needed.

Our Turmeric Curcumin has gone through extensive testing to ensure it's of the highest quality and purity available.

Fall Recipes

JACLYN RENEE'S

Green Smoothie Protein Muffins

2 BANANAS (RIPE)

½ CUP TRUVANI VANILLA PROTEIN POWDER

2 ½ CUPS BABY SPINACH

¾ CUP UNSWEETENED ALMOND MILK

1 TBSP BAKING POWDER

2 EGGS

1 TSP COCONUT OIL

2 CUPS ROLLED OATS

2 TBSPS PITTED DATES

RECIPE PROVIDED BY JACLYN RENEE

RECIPE DESCRIPTION:

In a world of grab and go, you can easily compromise quality. Also, wanting protein but always grabbing a smoothie can become boring. This is my take on a green smoothie but in a healthy muffin. Enjoy them for breakfast or as a snack with a cup of tea.

RECIPE INSTRUCTIONS:

Preheat your oven to 350° and line a muffin tin with parchment paper liners. Brush the liners with coconut oil, or use silicone cups to prevent the muffins from sticking.

In a food processor or blender, add baby spinach, bananas, Truvani Vanilla Protein Powder, dates, and milk. Blend until smooth, then add eggs, oats, and baking powder. Blend again until batter forms. Scoop batter into the muffin tin. Bake for 18-20 minutes, or until a toothpick inserted into the middle of a muffin comes out clean. Let cool and enjoy!

> " Many of my clients experience bloating from smoothies…the cold temperature makes it hard to digest. So, I wanted to turn the ingredients they put in a smoothie into chewable form. They are still getting their protein, fiber and veggies but it's in a fun, grab and go form.
>
> JACLYN RENEE "

AMANDA SCHUH'S

Salted Caramel Apple Smoothie

- 1 RED APPLE, CHOPPED
- 1 SCOOP TRUVANI VANILLA PROTEIN POWDER 
- 2 DATES, PITTED 
- 10 OZ UNSWEETENED ALMOND MILK 
- ½ CUP GLUTEN FREE ROLLED OATS 
- 1 TBSP ALMOND BUTTER 
- DASH OF SEA SALT 
- DASH OF CINNAMON 
- HANDFUL OF ICE

RECIPE PROVIDED BY AMANDA SCHUH

RECIPE DESCRIPTION:

This smoothie is a creamy, salty, caramel apple treat! It's also gluten free, dairy free and refined sugar free, so you can throw any guilt you might have out the window and indulge!

RECIPE INSTRUCTIONS:

Place all ingredients in a high speed blender, placing liquid first, and blend until smooth and creamy. Serve and enjoy!

> Hello, I'm Amanda. A stay at home mom, wife, and the creator of the blog, Healthymommamanda. Recently, I was inspired by the Autumn weather and started experimenting with a few fall flavors that I had in my pantry. The result was the most AMAZING Salted Caramel Apple Protein Smoothie using Truvani's, Vanilla Protein Powder. I really hope you get a chance to try this delicious smoothie because not only is it decadent but it's packed with protein, fiber, healthy fats, and other important nutrients. This smoothie has been a huge hit with every person who has tried it and I hope you have the same experience!
>
> AMANDA SCHUH

TRUVANI'S

Fall Harvest Salad Bounty Bowl

Bounty Bowl

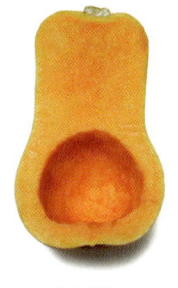

2 LBS BUTTERNUT SQUASH

1 ½ CUPS COOKED FARRO

1 TBSP OLIVE OIL

1 MEDIUM APPLE, CUT INTO CUBES

5 CUPS KALE, SLICED THIN WITH CENTER RIBS REMOVED

½ CUP DRIED CHERRIES

½ CUP TOASTED PECANS

SALT AND PEPPER TO TASTE

Dressing

2 TBSPS APPLE CIDER VINEGAR

2 TBSPS APPLE CIDER (OR APPLE JUICE)

¼ CUP + 2 TBSPS OLIVE OIL

½ TSP DIJON MUSTARD

½ TSP GARLIC POWDER

SALT AND PEPPER

RECIPE DESCRIPTION:

Quite simply, this bowl includes all things fall and all things delicious! Serve as a family meal on its own or as a holiday side dish. Serves 6-10 depending on portion sizes.

RECIPE INSTRUCTIONS:

Bounty Bowl

Preheat the oven to 375°. Peel and seed squash then cut into 1/2 inch cubes. Lightly toss in olive oil. Add salt and pepper. Place on a lined baking sheet and spread in an even layer. Cook in oven for 15 minutes or until roasted. Remove and set aside to cool.

To arrange individual bowls, start by adding a handful of kale to the bottom of each bowl. Add a scoop of farro to one section of each bowl and a scoop of butternut squash opposite the farro. Then fill in the rest of the bowls with remaining ingredients.

Dressing

In a small bowl, whisk all ingredients together and pour over each bowl. If preparing the dressing ahead of time, store in an airtight container and dress the bowl before serving.

RECIPE INSPIRATION

While everyone else is obsessed with all things pumpkin spice, we're obsessed with seasonal flavors and bounty!

SUSIE SANKEY'S

Salted Pecan Pie Bites

1 CUP RAW PECANS

1 CUP SOFT, PITTED DATES

1 TSP PURE VANILLA EXTRACT

¼ CUP PECAN OR ALMOND BUTTER

½ TSP SEA SALT

WATER, IF NEEDED

RECIPE PROVIDED BY SUSIE SANKEY

RECIPE DESCRIPTION:

This dish is the perfect combination of salty and sweet! It has a smooth, buttery salted pecan flavor with the perfect amount of sweetness. It makes for a great snack on its own or even eaten with a smoothie bowl or coconut milk ice cream!

RECIPE INSTRUCTIONS:

Combine raw pecans, soft dates, nut butter, vanilla, and salt in a food processor. Process until a uniform dough forms. If the mixture is crumbly, start with 1 teaspoon of water and combine until ingredients come together nicely.

Once the ingredients are all mixed together, scoop out 1-2 tablespoons of the dough and roll into balls. Arrange the balls onto a lined baking sheet. Place in fridge or freezer and allow to set about 30-60 minutes before serving.

Store in an airtight container in the fridge or freezer.

> " I love to bake and fall recipes are my absolute favorite to create and eat! I sell my baked goods at markets and I recenlty offered this recipe. I wanted to make something healthy that I knew everyone would enjoy. It was my best seller and everyone raved over them! "
>
> SUSIE SANKEY

JESSICA DILLON'S

Turmeric Ranch Dip with Veggies

Dip

1 CUP YOGURT OF CHOICE UNSWEETENED

1 TSP CHIVES
1 TSP PARSLEY

3 TRUVANI TURMERIC TABLETS, CRUSHED

1 ½ TBSP GARLIC

1 ONION, DICED

1 TBSP WATER

1 TSP LEMON JUICE

SALT AND PEPPER TO TASTE

For Dipping

CELERY

RADISHES

CAULIFLOWER

CARROTS

PARSNIPS

RECIPE PROVIDED BY JESSICA DILLON

RECIPE DESCRIPTION:

A healthy spin on ranch dip and seasonal veggies.

RECIPE INSTRUCTIONS:

Combine all spices, lemon juice and water with the yogurt. Stir until blended and it's time to dip!

> " Growing up, I was a ranch lover. I have always had issues with dairy and I also don't want to purchase processed ranch dressing at the store. This is a great alternative and it's so quick and easy to prepare! "
>
> JESSICA DILLON

ANJALI SHAH'S
Chocolate Macadamia Nut Protein Truffles

½ CUP WHOLE MACADAMIA NUTS

¼ CUP MEDJOOL PITTED DATES

2 TBSP MACADAMIA NUT BUTTER

¼ CUP TRUVANI CHOCOLATE PROTEIN POWDER

DASH OF SEA SALT

RECIPE PROVIDED BY ANJALI SHAH

RECIPE DESCRIPTION:

Made with just 5 ingredients, these truffles have zero added sugar but are still amazingly sweet and decadent! They're also double the size of their more sinful cousin, but only around 70 calories a piece.

RECIPE INSTRUCTIONS:

Add all ingredients into a food processor. Blend on high until the ingredients form a smooth dough.

Divide the dough into 15 equal parts (about 1 tablespoon each, maybe a little more). Roll with your hands into balls. Chill in the fridge for 1 hour (to set) before serving.

> " I grew up a "whole wheat" girl, but I met a "white bread" guy…when we got married, the question was: "What would my fast-food-loving husband and I eat for dinner?" I realized that the only way I would be able to bridge the gap between my husband's "white bread" world and my "wheat bread" world would be to cook healthy versions of foods that my husband enjoyed…so I taught myself how to cook and successfully changed my husband's eating habits from fast food to healthy, flavorful recipes made with simple, wholesome ingredients. In my search for a healthy, organic, protein powder free of heavy metals to add to his smoothies, I found Truvani!
>
> ANJALI SHAH "

JACLYN RENEE'S

Golden Milk Chia Pudding

¼ CUP CHIA SEEDS

1 CUP COCONUT MILK

½ CUP WATER

⅛ TSP CARDAMON

1-3 TRUVANI TURMERIC TABLETS, CRUSHED

¼ TSP CINNAMON

2 TSPS VANILLA EXTRACT

RECIPE PROVIDED BY JACLYN RENEE

RECIPE DESCRIPTION:

A fresh and healing take on the classic chia pudding with warming spices and turmeric for anti-inflammatory properties.

RECIPE INSTRUCTIONS:

Put all ingredients into a mason jar. Stir well with a spoon. Put lid on jar and shake vigorously. Place in the fridge to set and stir a couple of times over the next hour.

Enjoy after it thickens (about an hour) or make the night before for an easy breakfast.

> " I am always looking for healthy snacks and breakfast options that you can make ahead and grab and go. I love the classic chia pudding but I wanted to add a healing element to it like turmeric. "
>
> JACLYN RENEE

SARAH OWEN'S

Grounding Solstice Soup

3 YAMS

3 ZUCCHINIS

1 HEAD BROCCOLI

2 CUPS BRUSSEL SPROUTS, CHOPPED

3 CUPS MACADAMIA NUTS

4 TBSP OLIVE OIL

4 CLOVES GARLIC

SALT AND PEPPER TO TASTE

½–1 CUP FRESH BASIL, CHOPPED

6 CUPS FILTERED WATER

1 BUNCH GREEN ONIONS

RECIPE PROVIDED BY SARAH OWEN

RECIPE DESCRIPTION:

A creamy soup with sautéed veggies, fresh herbs, garlic, and yams for grounding. Perfect for warming you up and creating a digestive fire for the cool autumn months.

RECIPE INSTRUCTIONS:

Chop zucchini, green onions and garlic and place in a pot with 2 tablespoons of extra-virgin olive oil and 6 cups of filtered water. Bring to a boil and then simmer for 10 minutes. Allow to cool. Chop yams, brussel sprouts and broccol. Sauté in 2 tablespoons of extra-virgin olive oil on the stove on medium-high heat until slightly browned. Set aside. Put the zucchini, green onion, garlic, water and 3 cups of macadamia nuts in a blender and blend (I do it in small batches and pour each blended portion into a large pot as I go). This will create the soup base.

Bring soup base to a boil on medium heat. Turn heat to low and add sautéed veggies then bring to a simmer. Garnish with chopped basil and green onions. Salt and pepper to taste.

> " I wanted to create a nourishing soup without dairy, but just as creamy and satiating — and hitting on every flavor palette so that each bite is just as satisfying as the first.
>
> SARAH OWEN "

EMILY SCHIELD'S

Nourishing Lentil Curry

1 CUP DRIED RED LENTILS

1 CUP FRESH TOMATOES, CHOPPED

1 TBSP TRUVANI CHICKEN BONE BROTH

1 MEDIUM ONION, FINELY CHOPPED

1 TBSP GHEE

4 TBSP OLIVE OIL

3 TRUVANI TURMERIC TABLETS, CRUSHED

4 CLOVES GARLIC

FRESH CILANTRO, CHOPPED

1 TBSP LEMON JUICE

4 CUPS FILTERED WATER

1 TSP GROUND CUMIN
½ TSP GROUND TURMERIC
2 TSPS CURRY POWDER
⅛ TSP CAYENNE
1 ½ TSPS SEA SALT

RECIPE PROVIDED BY EMILY SCHIELD

RECIPE DESCRIPTION:

Warm up your body and senses with this satisfying lentil curry made with nourishing Indian spices. Simply delicious, you will want to make this heart-warming dish all season long.

RECIPE INSTRUCTIONS:

In a stock pot over medium-low heat, melt the ghee (or grass-fed butter). Add the onions and garlic, sauté until the onion caramelizes. Add the cumin, Truvani Turmeric tablets, curry powder and cayenne. Stir until spices become fragrant, approximately two minutes. Add tomatoes. Cook until the skin breaks down, approximately 5 minutes.

Rinse and drain the lentils. Add the lentils, bone broth and salt to the pot. Increase to medium heat and let the soup simmer for approximately 25-30 minutes, stirring often. Stir lemon juice into the finished soup and garnish with cilantro. Serve with raita and garlic naan bread for a wholesome dinner. Enjoy!

> " I was inspired by this recipe because I find Indian spices to be deliciously satisfying and nutritionally beneficial, especially because of the powerful anti-inflammatory curcumin. The briskness of fall weather brings me back to my stock pot as I crave to create nourishing soups. I adapted this recipe from my professor at Bastyr University, Cynthia Lair, author of *Feeding the Whole Family*.
>
> EMILY SCHIELD "

JACLYN RENEE'S

Instant Pot Cashew Chicken

1 LB CHICKEN BREAST

1 ⅓ TBSPS ARROWROOT POWDER

1 CUP CASHEWS

2 GARLIC CLOVES, MINCED

2 TBSPS KETCHUP

1 ⅓ TBSPS AVOCADO OIL

2 TBSPS RICE VINEGAR

¼ CUP COCONUT AMINOS

2 TRUVANI TURMERIC TABLETS, CRUSHED

3 TBSPS ORANGE JUICE

1 ⅓ TBSPS WATER

2 STALKS GREEN ONION, SLICED (OPTIONAL)

RECIPE PROVIDED BY JACLYN RENEE

RECIPE INSTRUCTIONS:

In a small bowl, add half the avocado oil, coconut aminos, ketchup, rice vinegar, orange juice, garlic and crushed Truvani Turmeric tablets. Whisk to combine. Toss the cubed chicken breast with half the arrowroot powder.

Turn on the pressure cooker to "sauté" mode. Add the remaining avocado oil and chicken then sear for 1-2 minutes. Press cancel and then pour the sauce on top. Set pressure cooker to "sealing" mode and cook for 10 minutes on high pressure (chicken should reach 165°).

While the chicken is cooking, whisk the remaining arrowroot powder and water in a small bowl. Carefully remove pressure cooker lid and add cashews and arrowroot/water mixture. Serve in bowls and garnish with green onions.

> " I always loved Chinese food growing up but after I became aware of all the preservatives, sugar and toxic ingredients, I stopped consuming it. I wanted to make a healthy alternative because chicken cashew was one of my favorites. It took some time to come up with a good sauce made from quality ingredients that had healing elements too.
>
> JACLYN RENEE "

ALISON HITE'S

Cheeky Clean Chili

14 OZ BLACK BEANS

14 OZ KIDNEY BEANS

14 OZ GARBANZO BEANS

14 OZ TOMATO SAUCE

3 ½ CUPS VEGETABLE BROTH

1 ONION

4 CLOVES GARLIC

14 OZ TOMATOES, DICED

1 SCOOP TRUVANI MARINE COLLAGEN POWDER

1 GREEN BELL PEPPER

1 JALAPEÑO

SEITAN OR YOUR FAVORITE VEGGIE PROTEIN SOURCE

PEPPER
SALT
CHILLI POWDER
CUMIN
CAYENNE PEPPER
OREGANO
A PINCH OF CINNAMON, TO TASTE

RECIPE PROVIDED BY ALISON HITE

RECIPE DESCRIPTION:

The easiest comfort meal for fall! This crock pot dream recipe is organic, dairy free, meat free and delicious! Plus it has a boost of nutrient packed ingredients.

RECIPE INSTRUCTIONS:

Chop vegetables. Drain and rinse beans. On cooktop, simmer tomato sauce and Truvani Marine Collagen Powder. Stir until blended. Add all ingredients to crock pot (except Seitan). Cook on high 2-3 hours or low 4-6 hours.

Add Seitan to a pan and sautée until warm, then add to crockpot and cook for an additional 30 minutes. Serve in bowls, garnish with cashew yogurt and hot sauce.

> I'm Alison from @thecheekyclean. I found it shocking how hard it is to find canned/jarred tomatoes or meat replacements without preservatives or chemical additives. I perfected this recipe with zero toxins for a healthy dinner (& leftovers) everyone can feel good & look good eating.
>
> ALISON HITE

DEBBIE HENDRICKSON'S

Sesame Mongolian Ginger Chicken

1 LB CHICKEN BREAST

2 TBSPS ARROWROOT POWDER

3 GARLIC CLOVES, MINCED

1-2 TBSP TRUVANI MARINE COLLAGEN POWDER

2 TSP GINGER, MINCED

¼ CUP CHICKEN BROTH

3 TBSP OLIVE OIL

⅓ CUP COCONUT AMINOS

2 TSPS HONEY

GARLIC SALT

SALT

SESAME SEEDS

GREEN SCALLIONS, CHOPPED (OPTIONAL)

RECIPE PROVIDED BY DEBBIE HENDRICKSON

RECIPE DESCRIPTION:

A modern Asian dish with a zesty ginger and garlic taste. EVERYONE loves it!

RECIPE INSTRUCTIONS:

Slice the chicken breast into thin slices. In a small bowl coat the chicken with garlic salt and arrowroot. Heat the olive oil in a large pan over medium heat and add the chicken slices. Brown for 4-6 minutes, until cooked. Set chicken aside.

Lower the heat of the stove to medium-low and add more olive oil if needed. Add ginger and garlic salt and cook for 2-3 minutes or until fragrant. Pour in coconut aminos, chicken broth, and honey and whisk to combine. Cook on medium-high for 2-3 minutes until the sauce thickens. Add Truvani Marine Collagen Powder and whisk until blended.

Add the chicken back to the pan and stir to coat well. Stir in the green onions and cook for 1-2 minutes. Garnish with sesame seeds (optional).

> " I have always loved Chinese food but never eat it anymore because of the soy, sugar and chemicals. So I made my own! I found other recipes and added my own healthy ingredients such as coconut aminos, honey, ginger and your Marine Collagen powder. This is probably my FAVE recipe right now.
>
> DEBBIE HENDRICKSON "

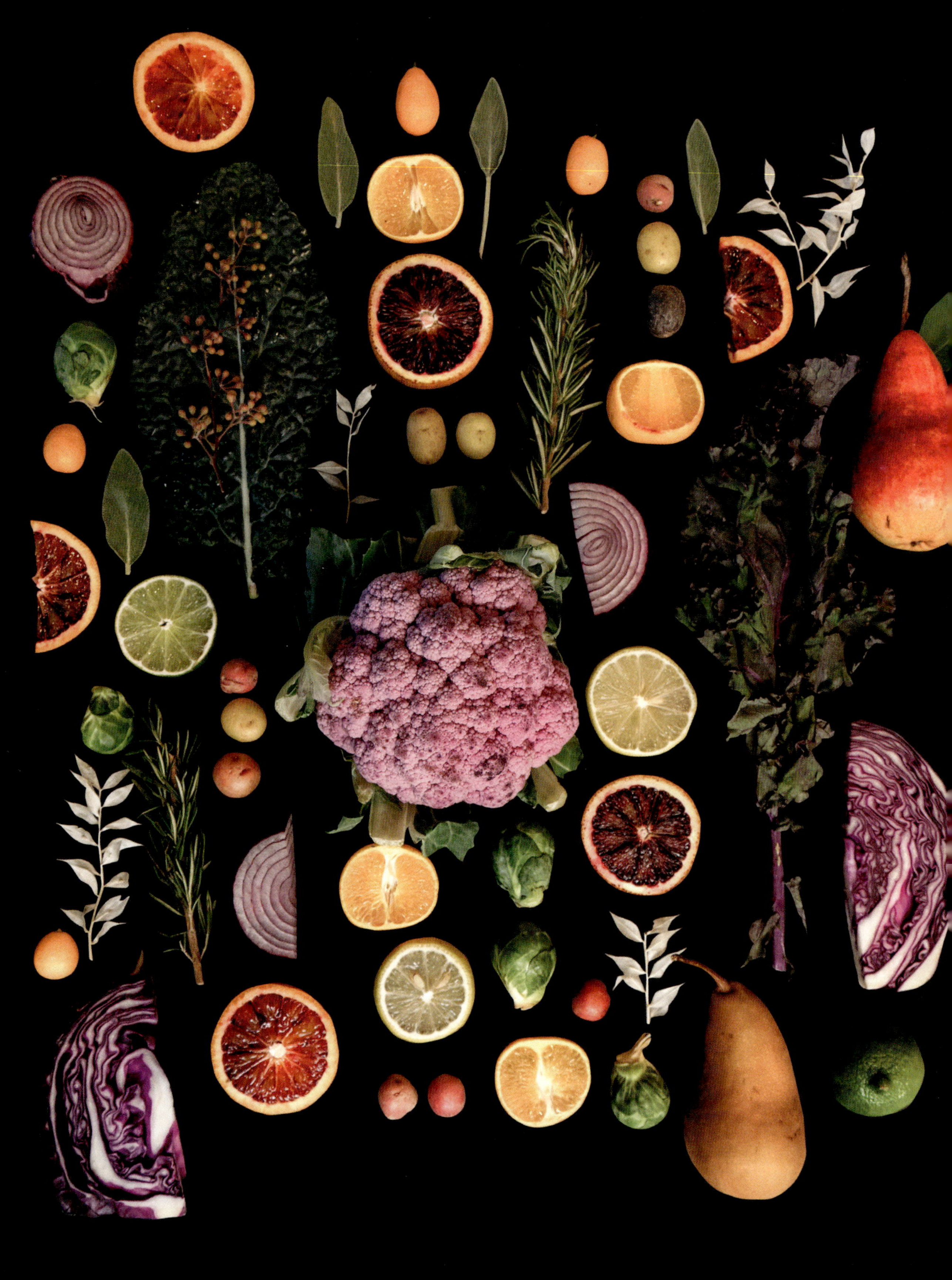

Winter

I am 100% committed to living and eating healthfully, so it may come as a surprise to many to hear that I love "comfort food".

But your definition of comfort food and my definition may be quite different, and I'm on a mission to change what "comfort food" means.

To me, comfort food is not junk food. Comfort food is warm and steamy, it makes me feel nourished, and it reminds me of things I enjoyed as a child.

Think stews, casseroles, and soups. All healthy. All 100% nutritious.

And when is the best time to enjoy comfort food? When the weather is cold and wet like it can typically be in the winter.

So it seems fitting that so many of winter's in-season produce work so well as ingredients into so many comfort foods.

Two of my favorites: Butternut Squash Soup & Sweet Potato Casserole.

There are some delicious comfort-food inspired winter dishes shared on the following pages. I am so inspired by the recipes shared by Truvani friends and customers, and I can't wait to get in the kitchen to make some of these.

xo,
Vani

DECEMBER
what's in season

Celery Root    Winter Squash    Kale

Potatoes    Lemons    Brussels Sprouts

Leek    Oranges    Turnip    Radishes

JANUARY
what's in season

Celery Root	Cabbage	Parsnips
Cauliflower	Broccoli	Turnips
Oranges	Collards	Kale	Grapefruits

FEBRUARY
what's in season

Turnips	Cauliflower	Broccoli
Tangerines	Rutabagas	Cabbage
Oranges	Leeks	Parsnips	Brussels Sprouts

Seasonal Spotlights

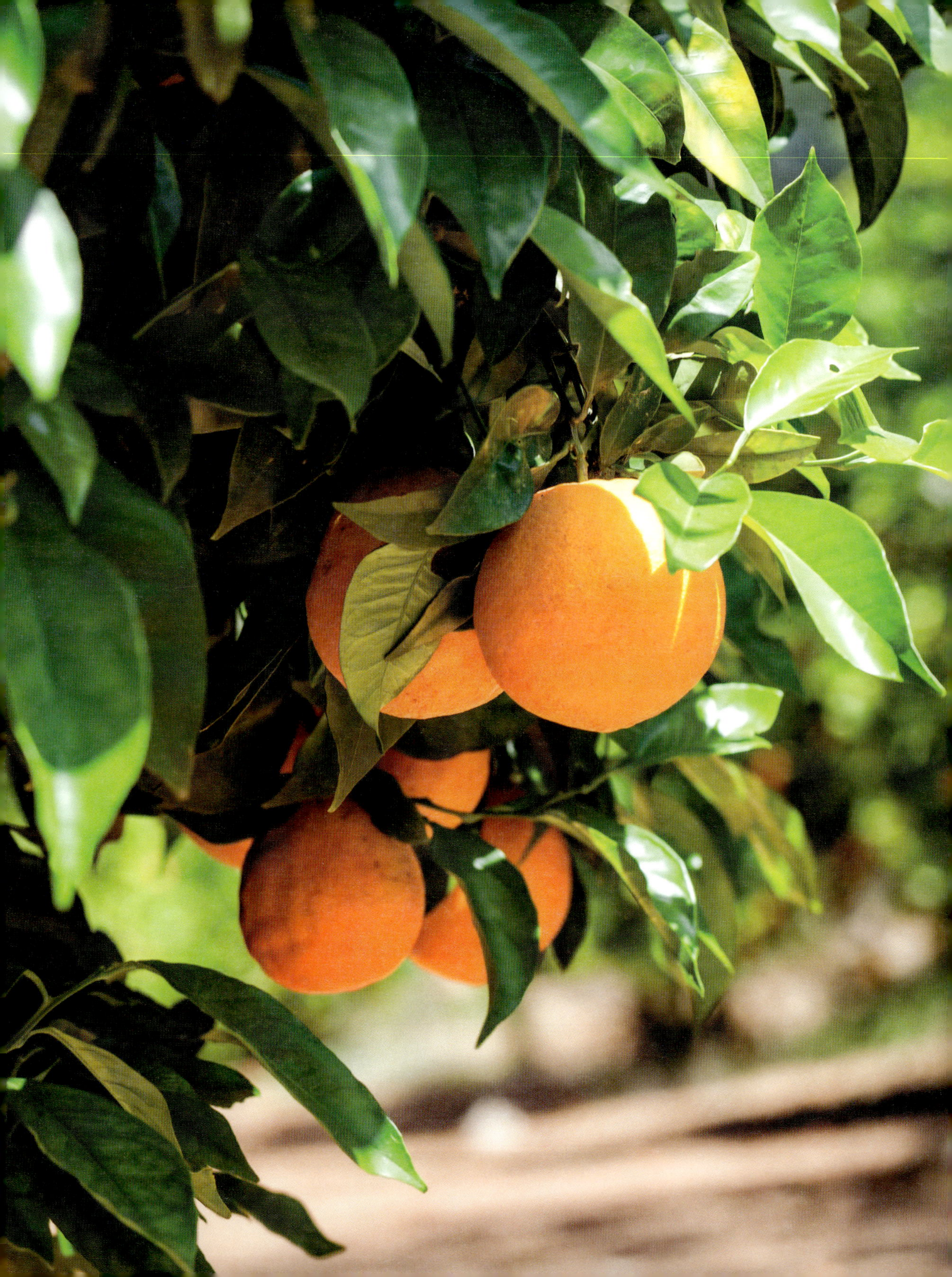

Winter Citrus

RATHER THAN FOCUS ON JUST ONE TYPE OF WINTER CITRUS FRUIT, WE WANTED TO HIGHLIGHT THE ENTIRE CATEGORY.

Why? Because we can't pick just one! Here are two of our favorites:

BLOOD ORANGES

Want a berry fix in the middle of winter? If so, opt for a blood orange. These globes of goodness, when perfectly ripe, taste like a sweet orange and a raspberry got together and had a baby!

The flavor is just one reason why you should grab this fruit in the winter. The dark fruit flesh color is a signal of a nutritional powerhouse - antioxidants. Specifically, Anthocyanin, a flavonoid known to help fight cellular damage in the body, which keeps us healthy.

KEY LIMES

We're singling out these mini limes from other limes for one key reason: guacamole!

Key limes are more tart than store bought limes, more aromatic with an almost floral note, and they make the best guacamole. Trust us on this.

But overall, limes are a healthy addition to your daily diet and lifestyle. Full of vitamins like C, magnesium, and potassium, add slices of lime to water, add flavor to your dishes, and make guacamole. Lots of guacamole.

Note:

Packed with nutrients and antioxidants, winter citrus fruits have so much to offer. Your skin will thank you, your digestion will thank you, and your immune system will thank you.

Brussels Sprouts

LIKE MOST KIDS GROWING UP, YOU'VE PROBABLY BEEN SERVED OVER COOKED AND MUSHY BRUSSELS SPROUTS.

Not the most pleasant of experiences, right?

When eaten out-of-season, brussels sprouts can carry a bitter taste, which causes most people to try and cook the taste out. This actually makes the bitterness worse.

When eaten in their prime—during the winter months—brussels sprouts are delightful! These mini cabbages can be sweet, aromatic, and are enjoyable raw as well as lightly cooked.

And brussels sprouts are incredibly good for you!

For one, brussels sprouts are high in alpha-lipoic acid, which can help lower glucose levels and increase insulin sensitivity. This means they can help fight and/or prevent diabetes.

Because of the high folic acid count, brussels sprouts are great for women during pregnancy.

They're are also packed full of nutrients, minerals, and antioxidants. And since brussels sprouts contain glucosinolates, they may also help decrease inflammation in the body!

So, next time you see a stalk of beautiful in-season brussels sprouts at the market, snatch em' up and eat em' quick!

Note:

If your brussels are dull in color, are yellowing, or have black spots – toss them out. Opt instead for brussels with tightly compacted leaves and are bright green in color.

Potatoes

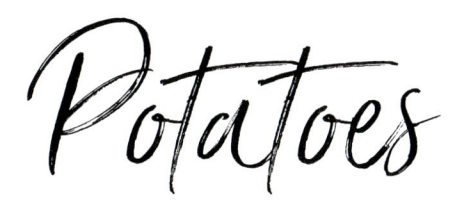

IN THE HEALTHY EATING WORLD, POTATOES GET A BAD REPUTATION.

It seems that yams and sweet potatoes share more of the spotlight in terms of being "good for you."

But the bad reputation is undeserved. Potatoes, when prepared properly, are incredibly nutritious and great for healthy eating.

It's just that most people assume they taste better when loaded with butter and salt, topped with cheese, or fried.

Potatoes, however, can be enjoyed healthfully. Add them to stews, casseroles, and even to your winter salads for an added boost of B vitamins.

In terms of B vitamins, potatoes are a powerhouse. Loaded with B6, potatoes have the ability to help fight disease, help protect the cardiovascular system, and help with athletic performance.

And while potatoes are abundant year-round, they are in season in the winter.

Note:

When preparing potatoes, it's important to enjoy them with the skin on since that is where a majority of their fiber is found.

Ingredients Matter

YOU MAY NOTICE A SMALLER SELECTION OF ITEMS AT YOUR LOCAL FARMER'S MARKET THIS TIME OF YEAR.

Without the long days of summer, and the warm sunshine that fuels photosynthesis, many of the plants and crops that feed us stop growing.

And they don't produce the food that feeds us.

So if plants are so affected by the sun, is it any surprise that we human beings are as well?

Just like plants use sunlight to photosynthesize, our bodies use sunlight to produce Vitamin D. The vital Vitamin D then helps protect our bones, helps fight various diseases, boosts our immunity, and can even help with regulating mood.

During the winter months when you're bundled in layers—or staying inside most days—it's especially important to ensure you are supplementing with Truvani's Vitamin D3 Supplement, Bottled Sunshine.

Whereas other Vitamin D supplements are made from extracting lanolin (aka "lamb lard") using a scouring process, washing it in detergent, and putting it through a series of saponification processes.

Our Vitamin D3 is extracted from a small plant species called lichen, making it 100% vegan.

EAT SEASONALLY

Winter Recipes

DAVID MEDANSKY'S

Steel Cut Oatmeal with Crunch

1 CUP WATER

¼ CUP OATMEAL

¼ TSP GROUND CINNAMON

¼ CUP WALNUT PIECES

1 TBSP GROUND FLAX SEED

1 TBSP GROUND CHIA SEED

RECIPE PROVIDED BY DAVID MEDANSKY

RECIPE DESCRIPTION:

Steel cut oatmeal made with chopped walnuts, ground cinnamon, ground chia seed and flax seed.

RECIPE INSTRUCTIONS:

In a pan, add 1/4 teaspoon ground cinnamon to 1 cup water and bring to slight boil. Reduce heat to low and add 1/4 cup steel cut oatmeal and 1/4 cup walnut pieces. Cook for 12 minutes. Stirring occasionally. While steel cut oats are cooking, combine 1 tablespoon ground chia seed and 1 tablespoon ground flax seed in a bowl. When the steel cut oats and walnuts are finished cooking add the ground chia seeds and flax seeds. Stir and serve immediately.

> " I like to get creative and figure out ways of increase ways of getting more nutrition into my meals. Also, I saw a comic of Dennis the Menace where in Dennis said, "I'll eat oatmeal when you figure out a way to get it to crunch."
>
> DAVID MADANSKY "

TRUVANI'S

Spicy Beet & Citrus Smoothie

1 SMALL RAW RED BEET, CHOPPED

1 BLOOD ORANGE, PEELED

1 CUP FROZEN MANGO CHUNKS

¾ CUP FRESH SQUEEZED ORANGE JUICE

1 CUP FROZEN BERRIES OF YOUR CHOICE

JUICE OF 1 LEMON

3 TRUVANI TURMERIC TABLETS

2 TSP FRESH GRATED GINGER

HONEY TO TASTE (OPTIONAL)

½ CUP POMEGRANATE JUICE

¼ TSP GROUND CAYENNE PEPPER

RECIPE DESCRIPTION:

When the days are short and cold, it's easy to start feeling run down. With this smoothie recipe on-hand, you'll feel like winter is on the way out, and you'll have a spring in your step in no time!

RECIPE INSTRUCTIONS:

Combine all ingredients into a blender and blend until smooth. Adjust the amount of honey and/or pomegranate juice to suit your taste.

TRUVANI'S

Winter Beet & Citrus Salad

Salad

- 2 BEETS, ROASTED OR BOILED AND CHOPPED
- 2 CITRUS FRUITS OF YOUR CHOICE 
- 2 CUP LOOSELY PACKED ARUGULA 
- VERY THINLY SLICED RED ONION FOR GARNISH 

Dressing

- 2 TBSP SHERRY VINEGAR
- 4 TBSP EXTRA-VIRGIN OLIVE OIL, DIVIDED 
- 1 SMALL SHALLOT, FINELY DICED 
- SALT AND PEPPER  
- 1 TBSP NUT OIL OF CHOICE (I.E. WALNUT) 
- ¼ CUP TOASTED PINE NUTS 
- 1 TBSP HONEY

RECIPE DESCRIPTION:

With arugula as the bed and beets as the grounding element, this seasonal delight gets all high marks. We love this salad for a number of reasons. It's beautiful, it tastes like an all night dance party, and it's full of vitamins and minerals.

RECIPE INSTRUCTIONS:

Put dressing ingredients into bowl: vinegar, honey, pine nuts and shallots. While whisking, slowly drizzle in olive oil followed by nut oil. Season dressing to taste with salt and pepper.

Coat beets with a portion of the dressing by tossing in a bowl before transferring to a serving dish. First put a bed of arugula down before arranging beets and fruits on top. Drizzle dressing on top of whole salad and then garnish with more pine nuts, orange zest, and red onion.

VANESSA CESAREO'S

Healthy Chocolate Chip Banana Protein Muffins

2 RIPE BANANAS

1 CUP ALMOND FLOUR

1 EGG

⅓ CUP CACAO POWDER

¼ CUP TRUVANI CHOCOLATE PROTEIN POWDER

¼ CUP COCONUT OIL (SOFTENED)

¼ TSP BAKING POWDER

2 TBS COCONUT SUGAR

⅓ CUP MAPLE SYRUP

¼ TSP APPLE CIDER VINEGAR

¼ CUP BUCKWHEAT FLOUR

¼ CUP OR MORE CHOCOLATE CHIPS

¼ CUP OR MORE PEANUT BUTTER CHIPS (OPTIONAL)

128 | EAT SEASONALLY

RECIPE PROVIDED BY VANESSA CESAREO

RECIPE DESCRIPTION:

A guilt free healthy snack or dessert.

RECIPE INSTRUCTIONS:

Preheat oven to 350°. Place paper liners in muffin tin.

In a large bowl; mash bananas, add egg, coconut oil, maple syrup, apple cider vinegar, baking powder and coconut sugar and stir well. Mix in almond flour and buckwheat flour. Add Truvani Chocolate Protein Powder and mix until blended. Fold in chocolate and peanut butter chips.

Spoon mixture into lined muffin tins. Bake for 12-15 minutes. Let cool.

Melt peanut butter and drizzle over muffins (optional).

> " Mommyhealthiest is who I am known as in this social media world and amongst people who are familiar with my lifestyle. My daughter, Luna was born seven years ago and I have chosen to raise her as organically healthy as possible. I also didn't want to deprive my child of all the tasty goodies that kids love so much. I began to focus on making healthy treats in place of the unhealthy junk food out there. It worked and is totally possible.
>
> VANESSA CESAREO "

TRUVANI'S

Roasted Cauliflower White Cheddar Soup

1 LARGE HEAD CAULIFLOWER

2 TBSP OLIVE OIL

1 CUP CHOPPED YELLOW ONION

3 CUPS WHOLE MILK

½ BUNCH OF CHOPPED FRESH PARSLEY

14 OZ OF BONE BROTH

3 ½ TBSP ALL-PURPOSE FLOUR

1 SCOOP TRUVANI MARINE COLLAGEN

3 TBSP BUTTER

1 CLOVE GARLIC MINCED

1 BAY LEAF
RED PEPPER FLAKES
SALT & PEPPER

¼ CUP FINELY GRATED PARMESAN CHEESE

1 CUP SHREDDED SHARP WHITE CHEDDAR CHEESE

RECIPE DESCRIPTION:

Roasted cauliflower is savory and delightful. Adding that roasted cauliflower to this creamy white cheddar soup recipe makes it one of winter's simple pleasures. Don't be surprised if this soup becomes a Sunday supper favorite. Not into dairy and cheese? No problem! Just swap it out with almond milk, and it still comes out creamy and delicious!

RECIPE INSTRUCTIONS:

Preheat oven to 425°. Chop cauliflower in uniform size. Toss in olive oil and coat evenly. Spread the cauliflower on a lined baking sheet, making sure cauliflower is not overly crowded. Season with salt and pepper, then bake for 25 minutes, or until golden brown and edges start to crisp. Remove and set aside.

In a large pot, melt butter over medium heat and sauté onion. Then add garlic and flour and stir until creating a roux. While mixing, add in milk and chicken broth, followed by parsley, bay leaf, seasonings and cauliflower. Bring to a boil, then reduce to low heat. Using an emulsion blender, purée until reaching a desired consistency. We like little chunks of cauliflower in our soup, but extra creamy is delicious too!

Finally, gradually stir in cheeses and mix until well incorporated. Season to taste and serve with a crusty bread.

STACEY ISAACS'

Pork Chili with Bok Choy

2 LB GROUND PORK

2 TBSP OLIVE OIL

1 MEDIUM ONION, CHOPPED

2 HEADS BOK CHOY, SLICED

1 RED BELL PEPPER, CHOPPED

1 CUP CHICKEN BONE BROTH

5 GARLIC CLOVES, CHOPPED

28-OZ CAN FIRE-ROASTED CRUSHED TOMATOES

1 TRUVANI TURMERIC TABLET

1 AVOCADO, DICED

3 TBS CHILI POWDER
1 TBS CUMIN
½ TSP CHIPOTLE CHILI POWDER
SEA SALT
BLACK PEPPER

1 SMALL HOT FRESH PEPPER, MINCED AND SEEDED

132 | EAT SEASONALLY

RECIPE PROVIDED BY STACEY ISAACS

RECIPE DESCRIPTION:

This chili has a great traditional taste. By adding bok choy and bone broth to this chili you are healing yourself in the most delicious and comforting way.

RECIPE INSTRUCTIONS:

Heat oil in a large pot over medium heat. Add pork and cook until most of the pink color is gone. Add onions, bell pepper, garlic, hot pepper, salt and pepper, chili powder(s), cumin, and Truvani Turmeric tablet. Stir until the pork is coated with the spices, continue cooking and stirring, about 5 minutes. Add can of tomatoes and bone broth and bring to a boil.

Add bok choy, cover the pot and reduce heat and let simmer for 20 minutes. Then uncover the pot and cook for an additional 20-30 minutes or until the chili thickens. Ladle into bowls and garnish with diced avocado. Enjoy!

> Football is huge in our house and chili is mandatory! Adding bone broth and bok choy to chili is a game-changer. The flavors are amazing and the healing benefits make this a win-win! And don't even get me started on the aroma that comes from the kitchen while this is cooking!
>
> STACEY ISAACS

STACEY ISAACS'

Creamy Apple Cider Vinegar Chicken

1½ LB BONELESS CHICKEN THIGHS

1 TBSP OLIVE OIL

1 MEDIUM ONION SLICED

⅔ CUP OF APPLE CIDER VINEGAR

1 CUP CHICKEN BONE BROTH

1 CAN OF COCONUT MILK (FULL FAT)

5 SPRIGS FRESH THYME

SEA SALT BLACK PEPPER

4 GARLIC CLOVES, SMASHED

RECIPE PROVIDED BY STACEY ISAACS

RECIPE DESCRIPTION:

This paleo, creamy, apple cider vinegar chicken is the most delicious way to incorporate bone broth and apple cider vinegar into your diet. The creaminess comes from mixing coconut milk with bone broth. This is the most comforting dish around!

RECIPE INSTRUCTIONS:

Heat oil in a large skillet over medium-high heat. Season the chicken with salt and pepper. Add chicken to the skillet and brown both sides. Remove the cooked chicken and set aside. Add onion and garlic to the pan. Sauté for one minute. Add apple cider vinegar and stir, scraping up any browned bits from the bottom of the pan. Add bone broth and stir. Return the chicken to the pan and add the thyme sprigs. Cover and simmer for 20 minutes, or until the chicken is cooked through (turn chicken halfway through). Remove chicken from the pan and whisk in the coconut cream. Let simmer for 5 minutes or until the sauce starts to thicken. Discard the thyme. Drizzle sauce over chicken and serve.

> " I am a chef with a Master's degree in Oriental medicine. I heal people with foods. I follow tons of amazing food and wellness bloggers, peruse cookbooks, and create healing recipes – this is what de-stresses me. I had a few clients who needed to incorporate both apple cider vinegar and bone broth into their diets and they needed a simple recipe that their whole family could enjoy.
>
> STACEY ISAACS "

ANJALI SHAH'S

Chocolate Vegan Chili

(1) 15OZ CAN BLACK BEANS

(1) 15OZ CAN KIDNEY BEANS

(1) 15OZ CAN PINTO BEANS

1 CUP FROZEN CORN

1 RED ONION, DICED

1 GREEN BELL PEPPER, DICED

1 RED BELL PEPPER, DICED

(1) 28OZ CAN CRUSHED TOMATOES

1 CUP VEGETABLE BROTH

3 TSP TRUVANI CHOCOLATE PROTEIN POWDER

5 GARLIC CLOVES, MINCED

1 HEAPING TBSP CHILLI POWDER
1 TSP CUMIN
1 TSP CORIANDER
¼ TSP (OR A BIT LESS) CAYENNE PEPPER
½ TSP SALT
½ TSP SMOKED PAPRIKA
½ TSP REGULAR PAPRIKA

½ TSP GARLIC POWDER

A COUPLE SPLASHES OF SOY SAUCE

136 | EAT SEASONALLY

RECIPE PROVIDED BY ANJALI SHAH

RECIPE DESCRIPTION:

This spicy, hearty chocolate vegan chili is so filling and delicious, it will satisfy vegetarians, vegans and meat-eaters alike! Protein packed beans combined with warm spices and a mole-like sauce make this the perfect winter dinner.

RECIPE INSTRUCTIONS:

Chop the garlic, onion, and bell peppers and set aside. Drain and rinse the black, kidney and pinto beans. In a stock pot, add 1-2 teaspoons of olive oil and sauté vegetables over medium-high heat. Add all remaining ingredients to the pot and bring to a boil. Reduce heat and simmer for 30 minutes or until chili thickens.

Garnish chili with anything you like: fresh diced tomatoes, green onions, avocado or tortilla chips all taste great!

> " I love how versatile Truvani Protein Powder is! Not only is it great for smoothies but I've started adding it to desserts, baked goods, and even curries and chilis! Which is where this recipe comes in. I wanted to create a healthier version of traditional chili that was still super flavorful, satisfying, and kid friendly.
>
> ANJALI SHAH "

FELISHA HENNESSEY'S

Cruciferous Dinner

BRUSSELS

PURPLE CABBAGE

BROCCOLI

WHOLE CHICKEN

BONE BROTH

SPINACH

CRUMBLED GOAT CHEESE

ONION POWDER

SEA SALT
CAYENNE PEPPER

GARLIC POWDER

RECIPE PROVIDED BY FELISHA HENNESSEY

RECIPE INSTRUCTIONS:

Cook chicken on low for 6-8 hours with 1 cup of bone broth. When chicken is done, shred with a fork and set aside.

Heat oil in a pan while you finely chop and add veggies to the pan. Start with the cabbage and brussels as they take the longest to soften, followed by broccoli then spinach. Once all of the veggies are added to the pan, season with salt, garlic powder, onion powder and cayenne pepper.

Add shredded chicken to the pan and toss together. Turn off heat, sprinkle with goat cheese (or any other favorite cheese) and serve.

> " I've been following Vani for years; she has truly inspired my organic journey and has led me to make so many healthy swaps for my entire family. The Cruciferous Dinner came about one day as I struggled to find a nutrient dense meal option at home and just threw whatever veggies were left in the fridge, into the pan. I was happily surprised at how delicious it was and have made some tweaks from the original to make it even better. I love how simple and nutritious this dish is.
>
> FELISHA HENNESSEY "

CHEERS TO YOU & CHEERS TO THE SEASONS!

Thank you for joining us on the journey to eat in season all year long.

Our hope is that the information, highlights, and recipes in this book inspire you to get out into your garden, visit your local farmer's market, and make something fresh and delicious for you and your family this year.

If you would like to connect with us,
please follow Truvani on Instagram or like us on Facebook.

ACKNOWLEDGEMENTS

This book would not have come together had it not been for our Truvani customers. We want to thank everyone who submitted a recipe for consideration. We look forward to showcasing more of your talents and passions in the year to come.

Special thanks goes out to the recipe contributors of this book:

JM MAXWELL	TEDDI VESEY	ANJALI SHAH
KEANI GENZEL	MARY TERDICH	SARAH OWEN
YOORI KOO	MARIANNA	EMILY SCHIELD
PORSCHE LACEWELL	JACLYN RENEE	DEBBIE HENDRICKSON
ANGELA REUTTER	AMANDA SCHUH	DAVID MEDANSKY
DEVRA STRUZENBERG	SUSIE SANKEY	VANESSA CESAREO
ALISON HITE	JESSICA DILLON	STACEY ISAACS
KELLIE SHIRLEY		FELISHA HENNESSEY

Recipes provided herein are for educational and informational purposes only and may not have been formally tested by us. We do not provide any assurances or accept any responsibility or liability with regard to any particular recipe's quality, originality, nutritional profile, or safety. You may not achieve the results desired due to variations in ingredients, cooking equipment, or cooking ability. We recommend that you use your best judgment when cooking, especially with any products, that when prepared improperly, may cause adverse reactions.

Copyright © 2020 by Truvani. All rights reserved.

No part of this book may be reproduced or used in any manner without written permission of the copyright owner except for the use of quotations in a book review.

ISBN 978-0-578-61735-0

Published by Truvani

TRUVANI.

www.truvani.com